THE HEART OF THE MATTER

Development, Identity and Violence: Reconfiguring the Debate

Edited by
Ravi Kumar

AAKAR

In Association with

ŠRUTI
Society for Rural Urban & Tribal Initiative

The Heart of the Matter
Development, Identity and Violence: Reconfiguring the Debate
Edited by Ravi Kumar

First Published, 2010

ISBN 978-81-935002-108-8 (Hb)

Published by
AAKAR BOOKS
28 E Pocket IV, Mayur Vihar Phase I, Delhi 110 091
Phone : 011 2279 5505 Telefax : 011 2279 5641
aakarbooks@gmail.com; www.aakarbooks.com

In association with
SRUTI
Q-1, Hauz Khas Enclave, New Delhi 110 016
Web : www.sruti.org.in
E-mail : sruti@vsnl.com

Printed at
Mudrak, 30 A, Patparganj, Delhi 110 091

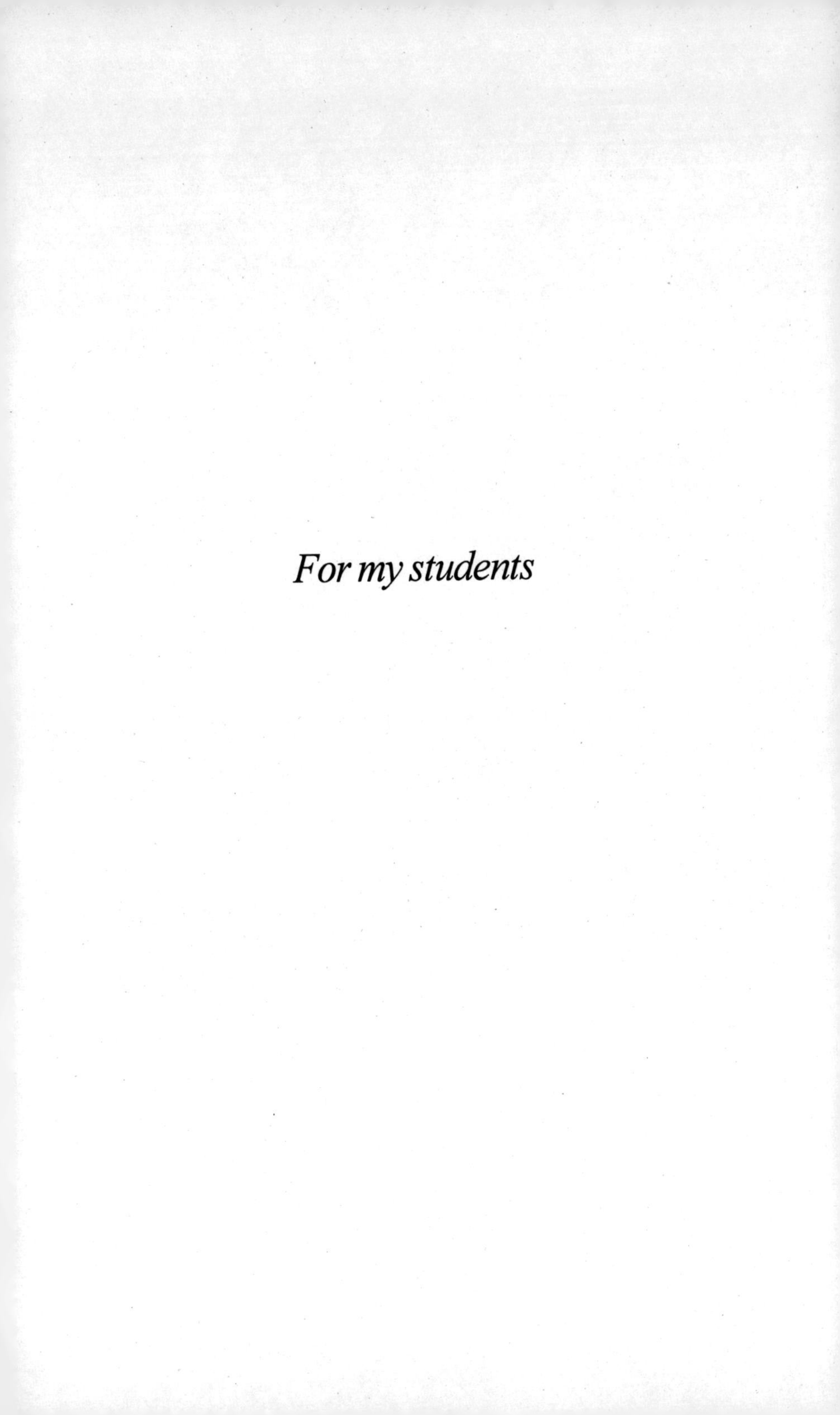

For my students

Contents

Acknowledgement

This volume is an afterimage of the first moment of what is potentially an act of redefinition and rebuilding; in addition, it represents the possibilities that constitute those who we call students — "those who learn, those who still need to learn". The volume is a defiance of this fundamental principle, even as we remind ourselves that "we are all students, always".

An initiative taken by the students of Department of Sociology, Jamia Millia Islamia, took the form of a seminar on "Contesting Development: Identity, Displacement and Violence", in January 2010. Papers were invited from students across universities in Delhi, abstracts were short-listed, and those selected were presented on the day of the seminar, where they were welcomed with incisive questions and comments.

This volume is made up of some papers selected from the ones presented, with an additional two papers written by faculty members from the Department of Sociology. The credit for organizing the seminar and for making possible the production of this volume goes, almost entirely, to the students of the Department — to Ipsita, Asim, Antaranga, Mubassir, Fahad, Himashri, Ramjit, Iqbal and Khabir among others. The faculty members — Neshat, Sheena, Savyasaachi, Kulwinder, Arvinder, Manisha, Azra, Gomti, Shareena, Pradyumna, Shakeel and Manoj — helped by their active support and participation. The seminar would not have been possible without the support of SRUTI and the keen interest shown by Rohit and Pravin. Lastly, I hope such endeavors continue in the future.

Introduction

Ravi Kumar

Glancing at the plethora of works produced in this direction over the last decade, d*isplacement* and *violence* seem the most popular characters of a much-debated, possibly over-debated area. Displacement has existed for centuries – for instance, kings would displace people from forests to convert the forests into hunting-grounds. But something about displacement today, makes it starkly different from the kinds that have existed so far. Perhaps, this difference can be understood keeping in mind the nature of modern nations which have emerged from the ashes of colonial empires, and have tried to ground themselves in the legacy of liberal democracy and the various other state-centric (people friendly?) paradigms of governance. The displacement of peoples from their areas of habitation under the garb of "development" can be seen across the history of Independent India; hopes of the people have been buried under the foundations of the "Temples of Modern India" which have been "constructed" one after the other, even as the state has continuously claimed to represent the interests of these very people. Of course, the nature and the degree of pretensions have changed, from the welfarist state to the neoliberal state. The continuance of unequal social relations, which is the founding premise of this entire setup, is the main cause of the displacement and violence we talk about, although this fundamental principle is manifested in myriad forms – from the economics of everyday-life to the politics of class.

The aspirations that force people to wage struggles, whether for national independence from colonial powers or against the tyranny of ruthless *zamindars*, or against the farce of the liberal-democratic state, have been subdued time and again through deft political usage of the idiom of *equality* and *justice* which are shown to be present just around the corner. While nobody denies their significance or the possibility of accessing them, one must not turn a blind eye to the protracted nature of the struggle that needs to be waged to attain them, a struggle that asks the systemic question of mode and relations of production. Can *equality* or *justice* be part of a system that thrives on accumulation of wealth through mindless profiteering and plundering of human and natural resources? We must explore the possibilities of altering the order of things, so as to put in place a system that does not only recognize the equality of individuals as social selves but ensures economic justice by ending private property.

During the course of struggle while identities define the lines along which mobilization takes place, as far as radical social transformation is concerned it is important to take into account the limits of identity politics. Identity politics which has side-stepped the dialectic of *recognition* and *economic justice*, has repeatedly been reduced to a mere mobilizational tool for the expansion of capital in recent times. One must analyze recent experiences, of movements and of confrontations with the neoliberal state, and see how the entire equation works. Such analysis of examples, where identities have been posited during the course of struggle, have asked questions of a radical nature, and then gotten co-opted by the neoliberal order can be found in the volume, especially in Chandra's paper.

The manner in which the state has put the natural resources of the nation out on sale, and has handed over trade to private enterprise, in policy and as "constitutional mandate" allows us to raise questions concerning not only the nature of the neoliberal state but also about the political economy of law. Legal institutions come across, as a result, not as "neutral bodies" but as instruments of the state, subservient to the interests of capital. The courts of the country have not only refused to taken cognizance of the displacement of millions of the tribal populace, but have also orchestrated the displacement of the poor from cities, to facilitate "beautification". These developments, for students of the "social sciences," have thrown up a wide range of debates like that of violence and the forms it takes, about the nature of the state (the peaceful state which forcibly uproots families, denying them their basic rights and the violent state which kills tribals and the common people to protect the interests of private capital in Kalinganagar or Narayanpatna), about the nature of resistance put up by the masses in Andhra Pradesh, Orissa, Bihar, Chhattisgarh or elsewhere, about the response of the state to such resistance, through orthodox "repressive state apparatuses" like the police or through militia like the Salwa Judum, and about the individual caught in collective and institutional manifestations of violence.

Violence, especially in modern times, comes across as the predominant mode of expression of the state – constantly demonstrating its presence. One of the papers, following Talal Asad, argues that "the state has not only been founded in violence, its political sphere has been maintained by the violent exclusion of slaves, women and foreigners" (see Badami & Nigam in this volume). This violence has not gone unchallenged, and responses, both violent and non-violent can be traced across the Indian map. People mobilize themselves to protest displacement, to protest police firings, to resist the terror of state-backed militia and so on; wherever capital moves, carrying with it the nationalist burden of the emergent bourgeoisie, it is resisted. But one must admit, that all resistance appears when violence takes certain identifiable, physical forms – on other occasions such tendencies have gone unchallenged in the last six decades, perhaps, because we cannot, or we will not, go beyond *appearances* to the *essence* of the problem

When trying to understand the nature of developments taking place in India in terms of state policy as well as resistance to it, the oft-repeated complexity of Indian society, in terms of presence of many sorts of identities, will have to be unwound. Keeping capital at the centre of analysis not only allows us to understand how identities are made to stand in opposing sides, but will also show how various terrains like those of the "social", the "economic", the "cultural" and the "political" relate to each other. In the final instant, there is more to the question of displacement and violence than the immediate and apparent human suffering. The tale of the vicious and inhuman, even anti-human, onslaught of neoliberal capitalism lies behind all this pain.

And then there is the hope of change, the hope of rebuilding what has been destroyed – this hope imbues energy into each mobilization that takes place for the sake of resistance. The discontent of the victims of violence, whose bodies tell their tales, express themselves in the violence of gun-battles as well as in the peaceful organizational strategies of countless organizations. Resistance throws up identities that express themselves radically against the grimness of their situation; then at a certain stage an identity congeals and develops aspirations to yield the power it had so far opposed. This is a process of constant flux, at least till the final battle is won, if not beyond it. This volume emerged out of an effort to understand these processes from different vantage points. It was also a product of an effort that was of a different sort – a forum where students came together, shared their views and debated over them.

1

Thinking through Urban Debris: Violence, Terror and the State

Nandita Badami and Anirban Nigam

I

The preoccupation of much of traditional western political philosophy has been the foundation of the state. For some of the earliest philosophers, conceptualization of the state went hand in hand with that of some form of the city. In effect, the utopia that was dreamt of, philosophized about, and in some cases empirically explored, was not just the state in the abstract sense in which we speak of it today, but specifically, a *city-state* (Mumford, 1965, p. 271)[1]. A sense of *urban-ness* was present at the heart of thinking about the state in political philosophy[3] that at times translated itself into images of a centre of civilization amidst vast agricultural and sparsely populated expanses and fortified cities (Plato, 2008; Machiavelli, 1964). While it is not our task here to trace a genealogy of such a connection, especially given that the early philosophers predated the concept of liberal democracy as well as 'urban' modernity, it is certainly the case that we witness a collapse of the state into the urban in the form our politics takes today. Such a statement needs qualification, and indeed, the links can be empirically established with a casual glance at our differential responses to contemporary crises in rural and urban areas. Urban crises (26/11, the Delhi bomb-blasts of 2008, the Mumbai floods of 2005) take the shape of *events*. While redressal of these problems occurs through the mobilization of state apparatus, there is a sense of urgency, a sense that *national* integrity is at stake. Responses take the form of calling not merely for state intervention in a sleepy, democratic, legislative manner, but demand swift, and sometimes openly authoritarian and surveillance-based resolutions: Unique Identity Cards, biometric systems, CCTVs. Rural crises, by contrast, do not take the shape of events so much as *processes* which go on (farmer suicides, caste violence and droughts). Responses take the form of calling for state intervention, but the notion of a threat to the integrity of the nation, and the sense of urgency that is felt during times of urban crises is missing. This collapse of the nation with the urban takes place through a "social relationship between people that is mediated by images" and other varied media found in modern society (Debord, quoted in Harris, 2007). The rural comes to be "othered" in a manner that makes rural crises removed from the centre of national politics, and state intervention in the rural qualitatively different from state intervention in the urban.

The assumption of urban-ness in the imagination of the state, both philosophically and in concrete contemporary terms, is incomplete without the question of the physical and moral defense of the new arrangement of society being addressed. With the arrival of modernity[2], the essence of the moral defenses presented in these theories became largely similar to each other: the morally independent individual's natural right to violent self defense was yielded to the state, and the state became the sole protector of individual liberties. The right to kill was abstracted from domestic politics, "denying to any agents other than the state the right to kill at home and abroad" (Tuck, quoted in Asad, 2008, p. 59). In this sense, one can locate a foundational violence, which has become an unquestioned and often disguised tenet informing our political thinking and social decision-making practices. In this section, we attempt to explore the effect of this underlying violence of the liberal-democratic state on forms of social living in modern cities, keeping in mind the almost intuitive relationship between the state and the urban.

Talal Asad argues in his book, *On Suicide Bombing*, that violence not only underlies the constitutive moment of liberal-democratic law, but the law thus established enshrines a particular *distribution* of violence that we then come to perceive as "just" (Asad, 2008). Certain forms of violence committed by the state in supposed defense of the rights of its citizenry are thus considered legal. Any violence that takes place "outside" the framework of the "just" violence of the state, disrupting its logic, is considered "terror," and is met with reactions of horror. (Suicide bombing, from this perspective, is an important disruption, for it is an instance of an individual "reclaiming" her right to violence as legitimate security *against* the state.) Asad's argument comes full circle when he points to the absence of this very horror as a reaction to *state* violence, indicating the regulation of the discourse on violence within the liberal-democratic system.

However, violence in liberal-democratic societies continues long after the theoretical-philosophical foundational moment has passed, and is an extension of it: The state is constantly engaged in producing and reproducing its liberal-democratic character through a series of acts of "mortal violence," repeated through history. Whether Athens or America, the state has not only been founded in violence, its political sphere has been maintained by the violent exclusion of slaves, women and foreigners (Asad, 2008, p. 59). Today, despite the abolition of slavery and the inclusion of women in the public sphere, the state finds other avenues through which to reproduce itself. The pattern of distribution of "just" violence, disproportionately invested with the state, produces an ideology which enables it to wage both internal and external wars against "threats," and enforce agendas of "development" that often do not even retain the pretence of representing a democratic consensus.

Additionally, it is also able to produce "horror" at violence committed by non-state actors which justifies extreme retaliatory actions.

Development that occurs internally, within a state, is related to its maintenance in two ways: first, the path of development chosen often re-enacts the foundational moment of violence, where the freedom of the "many" is ensured through the sacrifice of the freedom of "a few". A casual glance at many of the development projects in India serves up plenty of examples: Harsud, where an entire township was relocated in order to construct a dam; the massacre of tribals in Kalinganagar; and the spate of anti-democratic land acquisitions across the country that we have recently been witness to. Second, ironically, and almost directly contradictory to this, the rhetoric of development is also used to distance the state from associations with past violence, a process we shall term for our purposes here, the "externalization" of violence from the body politic.

Nowhere is the concept of externalization of violence clearer than in Gujarat after the riots. In 2002, soon after the pogrom concerns began to arise that the communal riots had affected the image of Gujarat as an investor-friendly destination. The state government's reaction to political pressures by Gujarati businessmen was to step up the profiles of summits held in order to attract foreign investment. In the post-2002 era, these summits went from being purely business summits to "extravagant government sponsored cultural events and exhibitions" (Desai, 2008, p. 11) – Gujarat, especially Ahmedabad, was literally "rebranded" (through campaigns such as "Brand Ahmedabad," launched in 2005, and more recently, the ad campaign for which Amitabh Bachchan has been signed on) as progressive, modern, and outward looking; efforts were made to portray the state as conflict-free and the 2002 violence as a thing of the past. Through the reconstitution and rebranding of the city, the government was effectively externalizing the violence, disassociating itself from it. It is interesting to note that the process of externalization went hand in hand with the reconstitution of the city as a modern, liberal and innovative hub of industrial capitalism. Today, the Gujarati middle class bristles at the association of Gujarat with the riots – for them, the fast-paced development that succeeded the riots symbolizes the "true" nature of the Gujarati state and people. They see no connection between the trajectory of events, beyond a quintessential liberal-democratic understanding that comprehends the events of the riot as the eruption of "primitive" tendencies, which have subsequently been overcome through development and modernization. There is something acutely *depoliticizing* about this ideology of development. The riot gets isolated, quarantined and temporally relegated to the past, leaving the present sanitized and ready to start "development" afresh. However, keeping in mind the violence inherent in the constitution of the liberal-democratic state, the relationship between Modi the Fascist and Modi the Modern Developmentalist, to put it polemically, appears somewhat more complex.

To begin with, there is a historical connection between state-sponsored ethnic cleansing of the sort that was experienced in Gujarat, and subsequent industrial modernization and political stabilization. This goes back to a claim that the originary moment of violence in the founding of states has taken the shape of ethnic cleansing of one form or another in many states of the West. Michael Mann argues in his book, *The Dark Side of Democracy*, that historically many European states, as well as America, produced a consensus of identity (a "mono-ethnic citizen body") through the process of ethnic cleansing. He argues that "murderous ethnic cleansing has been a central problem of our civilization, our modernity, our conceptions of progress, and our attempts to introduce democracy" (Mann, 2005, p. 4; p. vii). For Mann, the perpetrators of ethnic cleansing are not displaying attributes of primitive tendencies carried over from the past into the modern age; rather, these individuals and moments are created by conflicts *central* to, and characteristic of, modernity.

The argument that violence in our societies is a product of modernity, rather than the remnant of a more primitive age, can be inverted to create another aphorism: the trajectory of our "development paradigm", that is, the shape of our modernity, is produced by the violent edifice of the liberal-democratic state itself. Put into context therefore, the development trajectories of the state – created through a moral law that grants it the sole right to kill internationally and punish internally – are not surprising. This moral law, in effect, produces a context wherein the state is legitimately preoccupied with security, both internal and external.

This preoccupation – of the state with security – has a fascinating if somewhat under-theorized relationship with the nature of the development of cities. In recent times the physical security of the state has become increasingly linked to the security of cities – for instance, neofundamentalists (a term we prefer to use in place of "terrorist," explained in the second section of this paper) today strike at the heart of metropolises in order to strike at the heart of states. Stephen Graham has argued, in a different context, that urban planning is often akin to waging war, in that "ideologies of urban planning have often *invoked* metaphors of war and militarism" (Graham, 2004a, p. 174). We can develop this idea in two ways: first, the city as the "heart" of the state, needs to be secured physically against attack from outside and so is to be planned accordingly. In this sense, the need to protect the city from becoming a potential target for the enemy, dictates the manner in which cities are planned and developed. One instance of this trend can be found in Le Corbusier's work on cities in the 1930s. Corbusier was responding to the growing obsession with the protection of cities in the context of the development of increasingly sophisticated aerial bombs by the Great Powers. Cities before this time expanded with a congested horizontality, which offered themselves up as easy targets for aerial bombing.

However, one of Corbusier's most well-known inventions, the skyscraper, changed all this. Corbusier's idea was to envision the city vertically. This would mean tall buildings dotting vast, sprawling open "free spaces," making targeting much more difficult. Additionally, the height of a building was expected to protect residents from gas attacks by raising them above contaminated air. Some of his skyscrapers even came equipped with hardened, anti-aircraft, bomb-proof roofs (Graham, 2004a, p. 177). All of this is extremely ironic to note in our post 9/11 world, where the vulnerability of the sky-scraper has been graphically etched in our memories. No doubt the planning of cities will undergo further changes in response to new doomsday scenarios developed by futurists with ever evolving military and technological capabilities of states today.

The invocation of the metaphor of war in the planning of cities can also be interpreted to mean that cities must be secured and *ordered* against internal disruption, where the process of urban planning becomes the practical manifestation of the all important act of ensuring the stability of the state. The metaphor can here be further pitched at two levels: first, the militaristic vigor with which the state goes about the process of planned development – slum clearances, demolition drives etc – without being subjected to genuine questioning, the raison d'être giving it mandate enough, as in times of war. Second, the devastation of lives and livelihoods it leaves in its wake, which is often akin to the devastation and "forced resettlement" that occurs when a city is bombed in times of war (Graham, 2004b, p. 34). The violence of the state in such contexts appears, if not justified, then at least not as horrific and unacceptable as the massive urban destruction, and the devastation of lives and livelihoods caused by a neofundamentalist strike.

An additional aspect of the connection between urban planning and war, well explored by many urban geographers, reverses the relationship that we have been exploring so far. In this formulation practices of planning inform practices of war. Techniques of urban planning are used in order to maximize the "efficiency" of techniques of urban destruction central to modern warfare. For instance, in the United States during World War II, "model" Japanese houses were constructed out of both traditional materials (which were more flammable) and those which met newer "fire safety" regulations, in order to calculate precisely the quantity of explosives and time it would take to completely destroy Tokyo. Similar techniques were used to organize the "house-by-house demolition of Warsaw in 1945, set up the giant urban-regional process of the Holocaust, or starve many Eastern European cities and regions into submission in the mid-1940s" (Graham, 2004b, p. 34). It is even more unsettling to read that the planners involved in these processes, in some cases, went on to become extremely revered in their field. Graham speaks of one such case:

> "...the founder of Central Place Theory, that seminal economic geographer Walter Christaller – star of any traditional school human geography course...was employed by the Nazis to rethink the economic geography of an "Aryanized" Eastern Europe – a process directly linked to the planned starvation and forced migration of millions of people." (Graham, 2004b, p. 34)

It would hardly be an overstatement to say that since the industrial revolution, the city has been central to our imagination of modernity and progress. Even though tensions have always existed in the growth and spread of the western city, we still dream of modern, urban utopias (Vidler, 2002). To view the city as a modern utopia in this sense is, as in the case of Ahmedabad, a chronically depoliticizing position. As we have tried to elaborate in this section, the city exists at the crossroads of several forms of moral and physical violence. One empirical example of this can be seen in the fact that in recent years the city has become a site of increasing terror attacks – this is a theme we develop in the next section of the paper.

II

We attempt now to explore terrorism and how it acts as an "international language" (Beall, 2007, p. 4) that is constantly in conversation with developmentalism. Some caveats apply before we proceed. First, we are sensitive to the problems of labeling specific forms of violence as "terrorism". We accept also, that what goes by the name of "Islamic terrorism" in contemporary societies is neither specific to Islam (Roy, 2005), nor reducible to a fixed notion of Islamic culture (Mamdani, 2004). Keeping this in mind, we follow French sociologist Olivier Roy and use the term "neofundamentalism" instead of "terrorism". Although in this paper we focus on neofundamentalism of one variety, there is a specific reason for this – we wish to situate this form of deterritorialized neofundamentalism with respect to the territorial preoccupations of the state, and other forms of terrorism. Second, we do not believe that terrorism is restricted to the work of "non-state actors", and to this extent, reflect at some length upon the nature of state terrorism and how it engages with neofundamentalism and development.

If thus far, we have looked at how liberal democracies regulate violence *within* their own territories, we now wish to examine how violence is often extended beyond the boundaries of the nation-state. The city continues to be the major area of our concern. In the months and years following 9/11, a plethora of writings flooded the public sphere addressing the relationship between cities and terrorism. While many went somewhat over-the-top and predicted, for instance, the end of high rise buildings, others were more comprehensive in their reviews of the situation. In recent years cities across the world have become theatres of violence. This is true not only of cities in Europe and America, but also of the Middle East (Vidler, 2002) – and we might add, our own subcontinent. Archetypal instances of cities being razed to dust are of course the systematic bombing of Dresden, and the nuclear explosions in Hiroshima and

Nagasaki. More recently, we observe similar, if more gradual, destruction being wrecked on Palestinian cities, not to mention Baghdad and other war-torn urban locations such as Afghanistan. In contrast, cities like London, Madrid, New York, Delhi, Mumbai, Lahore and Karachi invariably experience violence that erupts suddenly, with no forewarning. These blasts scar the bodies of cities but seldom lead to extended reflections upon *why* such violence is being brought upon them.

Neofundamentalism is very much the product of a kind of globalization. In his study of resurgent religious movements, Olivier Roy argues that neofundamentalism is detached from any territory, has no social or economic program, and is, therefore, not interested in the state. Whereas institutions like the Church still believe their values to be universal and seek to implement them in society, neofundamentalism demands nothing from the state except for "abstention". According to Roy, neofundamentalist politics legislates for itself, not society – "the law is not good; it is the law." Moreover, neofundamentalism is an "agent of secularization" because, although the individuals drawn to it are not secular, they withdraw from a wider social world and (re)invent their religious lives in cloistered social surroundings (Roy, 2005, pp. 75-76). Contemporary neofundamentalism, Roy contends, is in many ways the heir of ultra-left "terrorist" movements of the 1960s and 70s. They draw on similar anti-imperialist rhetoric, and – fascinatingly – they stage their hostage dramas in tribunals that bear an eerily similar architecture to the peoples' courts among radical leftists of the past (Roy, 2005, p. 90). Elsewhere, he has written about the ways in which neofundamentalist movements plug into globalized "network society," how many who perpetrate violence today are second generation immigrants who seldom (if ever) undertake any political action in their country of birth or adoption (Roy, 2010). The fluid networks of these operations that Roy uncovers point to a globalized system at work.

We wish to contextualize this form of neofundamentalist violence in relation to state violence, by studying the urban scenario today. If the rhetoric of urban planning and "global cities" is a distinctly developmentalist-modernist one, then the desire to remake the world in the image of such global cities is merely and extension of such an ideology. That the developmentalist vision effectively destroys distinctions between "north" and "south" is clear enough from the fact that in India we speak less of London or Paris than of Shanghai. Perhaps, this is not a failure of imagination so much as the enunciation of our hidden desires to "develop" under the aegis of authoritarianism. Such homogenizing tendencies of globalization were what Jean Baudrillard called "the violence of the global" (Baudrillard, 2002). The Western world – and indeed parts of the East – seems to think that development is synonymous with urbanization. The process of urbanization, as we have argued earlier, is often akin to the enactment of war. When the US invades Iraq it not only "liberates" it, but it also paves the way for the *American* reconstruction of the country. Nothing illustrates this terrifying vision of a uniform world better than (the erstwhile?) Dubai, where the feudal-authoritarian vision of one man, who some call "the chief executive officer of Dubai," has transformed city into spectacle, crushing as far as possible, all voices of dissent (Davis, 2006). In this landscape of quiet, brutal, "progress" neofundamentalist attacks erupt as a chaotic challenge. Baudrillard wrote that terrorism is a perverse singularity because it is not a "counter-thought"; it defines the game and its rules (Baudrillard, 2002). It explodes without warning, in the middle of our urban utopias, opening up the wounds that constitute our everyday lives. In all of these ways, neofundamentalism mirrors the discourse of development. And as this game progresses, cities are but natural targets where the trophies of destruction can be made most visible.

Is the city then, a cherished target precisely because of the myriad of libratory ways in which it has been imagined?

Saskia Sassen has written recently, of the urbanization of war in cities, which are becoming battlegrounds for gang warfare, neofundamentalist attacks and "asymmetrical war". The most glaring and ongoing instance of the last type is Iraq where, as Sassen points out, the "war" was won in a matter of weeks, but the ground battles in Iraqi cities still rage on. One of the hallmarks of these attacks is their transnationality. Moreover, while traditional warfare required open arenas for rivals to fight in, today, cities have become frontlines in warfare of all sorts (Sassen, 2008).

Jo Beall, in an important essay, "Cities, Terrorism and Urban Wars of the 21st Century", draws parallels and divergences between the impact of terrorism on cities in the "north" and "south." Her approach to defining terror is useful, we think, for she focuses not on *actors* but on *acts*, thereby ensuring that acts of state terror aimed at cities can also be included under this rubric. She argues that while in recent work cities of both the first and the third world have been discussed, the latter are generally seen as "breeding grounds" for terrorists – an analysis which totally obscures the fact that southern cities are also victims of neofundamentalist violence, more so than the West one might say. (Needless to mention, this is a point we in India are also guilty of, blowing up our 26/11 to magnificent proportions but ignoring the almost daily battering of Pakistani cities.) If we look beyond this dichotomy, then we might find that the distinction between "developed" and "developing" is fast collapsing as urban areas in all parts of the globe come under various forms of terrorist attack. What is required is an analysis of the city in concrete terms. Beall argues that cities of the south are *more* vulnerable to terror – or indeed other forms of catastrophe – because it takes more time and resources for these parts of the world to recover from great damage. This obviously affects the larger development patterns of cities that are attacked. In other words, while the risks associated with terrorism are not very dissimilar in the north and south, the "outcomes" are significantly different (Beall, 2007, p. 11).

In both the north and the south however, attacks on the city – what some scholars are now calling "urbicide" – is increasingly becoming an instrument of state terrorism. Martin Coward has analyzed the function of urbicide during the war in Bosnia in the 1990s. In that war, Coward contends, a great amount of the violence was not "collateral" but in fact, precisely directed at urban structures – architecture and spaces that symbolized ethnic heterogeneity and cosmopolitanism. Eyal Wiezman's focus on the "*developmental* side" of the Israel-Palestine conflict shows how, through "'security' barriers, bulldozed 'buffer zones', fortified new Jewish settlements, new Jewish-only roads, and besieged Palestinian cities", Israel has initiated a phase of urban war which makes the functioning and continuation of the Palestinian state increasingly difficult. Stephen Graham's work too shows how these Israeli initiatives lead to, apart from other things, the "*demodernization*" of the Palestinian urban infrastructure (Graham, 2004b, pp. 138-9). During the 1990-91 Gulf War Gautam Banarji wrote that American assaults on Baghdad's urban landscape reduced what was a fairly modern city to a "pre-industrial age" (Beall, 2007, p. 16).

We have argued in this paper that the discourse of development in liberal-democratic states cannot be extricated from the larger histories of violence that constitute these states. One current of the present ideology of globalization endeavors to "flatten" the world and produce cities from conveyer belts. It expects the world to forsake all that appears aberrant and step into the splendid glory of modernity. This vision of developmentalism imagines a world without differentiation, where what the West has labeled "under-developed" must be brought up to speed with the world around it. Jean Baudrillard's claim that the violence of the global has taken over from the death of the universal seems all the more true in a context where human rights and other such slogans are caricatured in enterprises like war and subsequent reconstruction of states. Neofundamentalism, we have argued, is in perverse dialogue with this ideology of progress – although, it is in many ways intimately linked to it. Sporadic, random, non-state violence detonates across location and time, killing blindly whoever stands in the way. Ultimately, both visions aim at spatio-temporal conquest, seeking to make a world in their own image. Both play by their own rules in a game where the body count becomes an afterthought. If this emerges as sharper and clearer in the case of neofundamentalism then we have only ourselves to blame; for in our clamber to the top of the world we have overlooked the tremendous – if more gradual – violence that is occurring all around us. We are not, here, "comparing" two forms of violence. Nor are we making ethical judgments either, to the extent that one can actually talk about phenomena such as these without a sense of the ethical. Our attempt has neither been to reduce neofundamentalism to a single dimension, nor make a case for the hopelessness of any form of developmentalism within the framework of the state. Rather, we have selected two forms of violence that we think are increasingly defining our lives, and have attempted to understand both in a context where the strict binaries of the developmentalist world no longer hold.

III

This "postscript" seeks to address a couple of questions which came up during the seminar at Jamia Millia Islamia where our paper was presented. One question, posed to us, concerned a "comparative evaluation" of Maoist and neofundamentalist violence. The other, raised throughout, had to do with alternatives to the present situation. In this section we want to revisit our most fundamental argument about the state, and tackle the question of ethics that we disavowed above, from a different angle. It is our understanding that once we demonstrate that the liberal-democratic state is constituted by violence, the normative demands we make to the state as part of social and political movements, no longer stand in the simple and unproblematic way in which they might have before. Stressing on the repressive apparatus of the state could also suggest that we wholeheartedly support *all* forms of resistance against the state, since we can no longer make any assumptions about what a state "should" do.

In trying to unravel this question, we turn our attention to a specific aspect of the contemporary Maoist movement in India, an aspect we feel has not been adequately addressed in recent debates on "Left Wing Extremism". Specifically, the object of our analysis is the *mediatization* of the Maoist movement and how, in the process, constructions of a rural-urban binary have dissolved in much the same way that the binaries of the developmentalist world have collapsed. The Maoist movement's engagement with the urban can be seen in three stages, through three events. The first is a document widely available on the internet. It is titled *Urban Perspectives* and outlines a "plan of action" for Indian cities in the years to come[4]. The document, dated 2007, seeks ultimately to draw urban support for the "people's war" being waged in rural India. Its imagination of the urban (the word "megacity" appears from time to time) produces a layered and complicated map. Everything – from class structure to the spatial organization of the city and the infinite varieties of civil society groups active in them – is considered. Towards the end of the document even "cyberwar" gets a mention. What we wish to highlight is precisely this attempt to engage with the urban, even if on somewhat unsure footing, and co-opt it into the agenda of a secret anti-state movement, the heart of which is still, arguably, the rural.

With the arrest of Kobad Ghandy in Bhikaji Cama Place in Delhi, suddenly Maoist presence in the city became more corporeal. Investigations after his arrest spoke of a network he was a part of, which disseminated Maoist propaganda in urban locations (*Hindustan Times*, February 21, 2010). Barely had this second moment receded from the headlines when what some are calling "Operation Green Hunt" began. Or the hysteria around it did. In the past few months, press conferences, meetings, discussions, and demonstrations have colonized urban space and thrust cities like Delhi to the forefront of the anti-Green Hunt movement. The rhetoric of state repression and silencing of dissent is now a properly urban rhetoric where the rural hinterland is no longer an actually existing place, but almost a literary device in the charges and counter-charges being traded by all sides. At the centre of this theatre is the shadowy figure of Kishenji, who has been propelled in a matter of months, from the tribal areas of West Midnapore to the television studios of local and national news channels. He gives interviews in electronic and print media commenting on the present crises, writes replies to human rights activists from his hideout in the forest, stages mediatized "P.O.W." exchanges, and, bypassing the General Secretary of his party, offers ceasefires to the government. Kishenji's rise as media performer is nothing if not a testimony to the power of the urban and the mobility of ideas made possible through technology. Without a cell-phone he would be non-entity. Without Delhi or Kolkata he would have nowhere to preach to. With his confident mastery the technologies of media he has catapulted a rural movement to the centre of the urban imagination; and as the Indian state has prepared to march into Dandakaranya, Dandakaranya has been marching towards Delhi. There is a fascinating paradox in all of this of course, for while the Maoists in their self-presentation produce an undifferentiated category of "people" or "tribals" that have been victimized and terrorized by the state, the corporate media's attempt to represent tribals produces an undifferentiated category of "Maoists".

Our interest however, lies elsewhere. What these rapid developments demonstrate with great clarity is the impossibility of thinking of the state without the city. The city is the space where, it seems, *all* discontent must be articulated. The symbolic presence of the city on the national landscape ensures that without the support of urban personalities, "rural" causes become almost meaningless. This is of course, an imagined construction, but an important one. Still, not everyone addresses the city on the same terms.

Neofundamentalist violence *disrupts* the city; it breaks the monotony of everyday existence with spectacular displays of random violence. Maoist visions of the city are however, rather different. On the one hand their recent move towards the city comes with the realization of the importance of the urban to contemporary Indian politics. At the same time, unlike neofundamentalism Maoism has a stake in the system – it doesn't wish to simply disrupt daily life; it wishes to *capture* the city.

It is at this level that we would like to speak of alternatives. Needless to say, the Maoist desire to "capture" the city is a pipe dream. But what we are concerned with here are the terms in which challenges to the state are voiced. Ideologies which seek to capture power and *become* the state merely create an alternative structure of oppression and violence. Our argument about liberal-democratic states can, then, be reformulated in the following manner: it is not the liberal-democratic state alone with which we are taking issue, but *the state as such*. In our reading therefore, no emancipatory project driven by a vanguardist organization can arrive at something "better" than the present order. As Kropotkin said aptly over a century ago, "we have already had too much of Jacobin utopias!" (Kropotkin, 2008, p. 80) It is also worth highlighting that ostensibly revolutionary movements like the Maoists' do not, in our opinion, have any understanding of what they dismiss often as "bourgeois democracy." While the main thrust of our paper has been to uncover a different story of liberal-democratic states, we believe firmly that *any* resistance to the state must be articulated in democratic terms. The tenets of the "New Democratic Revolution" as they are presented to us today do not satisfy such a condition. Secrecy, vanguardism, and the *programmatic use of armed resistance* are not commensurate with the "democracy" speak of.

Our purpose here is to explicitly refuse to outline an "alternative" to the options currently before us. The desire for easy alternatives appears more often than not, to be a search for formulaic answers which traverse complex histories with comfortable confidence. When we argue that organizations like the CPI(Maoist) do not understand bourgeois democracy, we do so with something very specific in mind. For although we have spent our entire paper attempting to open up the violent edifice of liberal-democracies, it would be foolish on our part to assume that this is the only story to tell. Our political project – if we dare call it that – lies in identifying ruptures and fissures, in trying constantly to destabilize what appears as stable. We cannot therefore produce a narrative of liberal-democracy as simply a form of totalitarianism. That democratic regimes are repressive and violent might be true, but they exist constantly under the threat of their own normative ideals. In this sense, the possibility of perforation is ever-present; and herein lies the truth of what Claude Lefort has famously identified as the "empty space of power" in democracy (Laclau and Mouffe, 2001, p. 186). François Furet too was sensitive to the importance of this aspect of the French Revolution. In spite of his piercing critique of Jacobinism and state terror, Furet reaffirmed continuously the fact that something had changed fundamentally with the events of the revolution (Furet, 1981). One can only add here that the *idea* of democracy is not, we would like to think, a liberal monopoly. For us then, Laclau and Mouffe's theorization of "radical democracy" is crucial because it resists the temptation of many revolutionary theories (the latest of which is probably Hardt and Negri's conception of the "multitude,") to assimilate various strands of challenges to the state under one – even if amorphous – banner. Such views end up producing unproblematic alliances between movements that might not coexist with great comfort. What we want to re-emphasize is the *heterogeneity* of both state and anti/non-state practices, heterogeneity without which we miss the fundamental complexity and contradiction of liberal-democracy, and without which we seek always to produce *coherence* in challenges to the state. As we negotiate these cycles of violence and counter-violence we might do well to contemplate the potential of symbolic and poetic interruptions of the everyday. Here, the following imagination of "direct action" by an anarchist collective, Crimethinc.[5], is perhaps apt to close our discussion:

> ...[W]e need to invent new games—games that can take place in the conquered spaces of this world, in the shopping malls and restaurants and classrooms, that will break down their proscribed meanings so that we can give them new meanings in our accordance with our own dreams and desires. We need games that will bring us together, out of the confinement and isolation of our private homes, and into public spaces where we can benefit from each other's company and creativity. Just as natural disasters and power outages can bring people together and be exciting for them (after all, they do make for a little thrilling variety in an otherwise drearily predictable world), our games will join us together in doing new and exciting things. We will have poetry in the factories, concerts in the streets, sex in the fields and libraries, free picnics in supermarkets, public fairs on freeways.

Endnotes

1. Mumford makes this point in relation to the Hellenistic philosophers.
2. We use the word *urban-ness* here to invoke the vision of utopia rooted specifically in the social arrangements of a city that Mumford speaks of as characteristic of the Hellenistic philosophers. The centrality of the city in the envisioning of the state can also be seen later in pre-modern times, in philosophers like Machiavelli. Although Machiavelli's preoccupations were a far cry from utopian, the imagination of the state was for him rooted in the city and thus in a form of urbanism, as well. Indeed, the origins of the word date back to this period.
3. Commonly taken in political philosophy to begin with the works of Hobbes.
4. This document was published in 2007 and is available at http://maoistresistance.blogspot.com/2007/10/cpi-maoist-urban-perspective.html

5. This work is available at http://www.crimethinc.com/texts/atoz/alienation.php

References

Asad, T. (2008). *On Suicide Bombing*. Kolkata Seagull.

Baudrillard, J. (2002). The Violence of the Global. [http://www.egs.edu/faculty/jean-baudrillard/articles/the-violence-of-the-global]

Beall, J. (2007). Cities, Terrorism and Urban Wars of the 21st Century. *LSE Crisis States Working Papers Series No. 2, Working Paper No. 9.*

Crimethinc. (Undated) AlieNation: The Map of Despair: Space/Time Control, Space Travel, and Space Exploration. [http://www.crimethinc.com/texts/atoz/alienation.php]

Davis, M. (2006). Fear and Money in Dubai. *New Left Review 41, September-October.*

Desai, R. (2008). Urban Landscapes of Hindutva: Reshaping Urban Space and Redrawing Citizenship in Ahmedabad, India. *"Cities and Fundamentalisms", Woodrow Wilson International Center for Scholars, Washington DC, Aug 15-16, 2008.*

Furet, F. (1981). *Interpreting the French Revolution*. Cambridge: Cambridge University Press.

Graham, S. (2004a). Postmortem City. *City: Analysis of Urban Trends, Culture, Theory, Policy, Action,* Vol. 8, No. 2, July 2004.

Graham, S. (2004b). Cities as Strategic Sites: Place Annihilation and Urban Geopolitics. In Graham S. (Ed.) *War, and Terrorism: Towards and Urban Geopolitics*. Oxford: Blackwell.

Graham, S. (2004). Urbicide and the Urbanization of Warfare: Introduction. In Graham S. (Ed.) (2004) *War, and Terrorism: Towards and Urban Geopolitics.* Oxford: Blackwell.

Harris, Z. (2007). Spectacle. [Available at: http://csmt.uchicago.edu/glossary2004/spectacle2.htm]

Kropotkin, P. (2008). *The Conquest of Bread*. BiblioBazaar, LLC.

Laclau, E. and Mouffe, C. (2001). *Hegemony and Socialist Strategy: Towards a Radical Democratic Politics (Second Edition)*. London: Verso.

Machiavelli, N. (1964). *The Prince and Other Works*. Hendricks House.

Mamdani, M. (2004). *Good Muslim, Bad Muslim: America, the Cold War, and the Roots of Terror*. Ranikhet: Permanent Black.

Mann, M. (2005). *The Dark Side of Democracy: Explaining Ethnic*

Cleansing. Cambridge: Cambridge University Press.

Mumford, L. (1965). Utopia, City and the Machine. *Daedalus, Vol. 94, No. 2, Utopia.*

Plato, (2008). *Laws*. New York: Cosimo.

Roy, O. (2005). *Secularism Confronts Islam*. New York: Columbia University Press.

Roy, O. (2010). The Allure of Terrorism. *New York Times, January 10, 2010.*

Sassen, S. (2008). The New Wars and Cities: Something is Changing. *The Huffington Post, November 26, 2008.*

Vidler, A. (2002). A City Transformed: Designing "Defensible Space". *Grey Room, No. 7, On 9/11.*

2

Through and Beyond: Identities and Class Struggle

Paresh Chandra

The New and the Primitive: the New is the Primitive

I

In India, the effectuation of the New Economic Policy in 1991 is seen as a move forward, a move out of the "mires" of public sector enterprise, a "mandate" for privatization and against public and state ownership of industries. It is a short-sightedness characteristic of our times, our inability, Fredric Jameson would say, to historicize, which speaks when we make such utterances. Unable to look beyond the immediate we are unable also to make logical generalizations and connections that are needed to contextualize what occurs. Before putting forth my arguments I feel the need to make two assertions: (1) The NEP was not adopted because 'Plan 1, public sector,' failed (2) state ownership does not mean public ownership, and hence the seeming failure of public sector enterprises is by no means evidential of the problems of truly collective ownership of means of production.

Historians have noted that 'at the eve of Independence' the Indian bourgeois class was much more developed than that of most third world nations. Post 1910 the British government had begun to include the interests of this class in its policies, partly because of its own compulsions (the British needed the support of the Indian bourgeoisie in World War I) and partly because of strength of this class (Mukherjee, 2002). Subsequently, the plan of development that was charted out centrally after Independence had to accommodate the said interests as well. In 1944-45 when prominent capitalists sat down to ponder the possibilities facing an Independent India, and divined the Bombay Plan, they knew that they were going to have a very big say in the path the country takes. As a result of underdeveloped infrastructure, it seemed convenient to Tata, Birla and Co. to lay out an arrangement which required the state to make all necessary large investments, before they take over. To overstate for rhetorical effect, the next thirty years fulfilled the wishes of the Indian capitalist class. Of course, the Bombay Plan was never actually followed, but the 'development' that ensued in these years was more or less in concert with it. In the 80s, even as the judiciary's earlier attempts to strengthen labour laws and expand the purview of Constitutional provisions like the "Right to Life" took a down turn, the state continued with this construction of infrastructure, at the same time beginning to prepare for the change of hands that was finalized in 1991. From state capitalism to privatization in the age of neoliberalism – this has been the movement of the Indian socio-economic formation. So, we might as well stop arguing about this "development paradigm," for its "theoretical underpinnings" and its genealogy are clear enough: contesting this development is without a doubt, contesting capitalism.

Neoliberalism, the stage of finance capitalism, even as it (as will be discussed later) uses direct dispossession to accumulate capital, is also the most decentralized and dispersed form of capitalism. As Jameson observes in his essay "The Cultural Logic of Late Capitalism" the magnitude of this system and the manner in which it operates is such that one cannot find a centre to it, and it becomes impossible to locate a dominant form to understand or attack. It is capable of assimilating and preserving local forms and identities, which it brings together in relationships or 'networks' of competition. Due to the absence of a dominant form of hegemony, of a monolithic state, it becomes impossible to think of a universally valid form for struggle. The problem of "identities" the way it exists in the current conjuncture, where many of them coexist, all equally subordinated to the rule of capital, and without palpable partiality on part of the state, is one that is borne off this situation. Identities are forced to compete in the networks created by the generalization of capital that has brought neoliberalism. In this situation it is hard to believe in grand-narratives; since identities coexist, interests appear relative, none seems to have a greater claim to authenticity than any other – the schizophrenia of the postmodern subject is what we get. The internationalism of neoliberalism, together with its ability to preserve and force identities into competitive relations, makes it hard to conceive of a transcendental politics; and the harder it is, the greater the need to envision it. Jameson (1991, p. 49) says:

> ...the as yet untheorized original space of some new "world system" of multinational or late capitalism, a space whose negative or baleful aspects are only too obvious – the dialectic requires us to hold equally to a positive or "progressive" evaluation of its emergence, as Marx did for the world market as the horizon of national economies, or as Lenin did for the older imperialist global network. For neither Marx nor Lenin was socialism a matter of returning to smaller (and thereby less repressive and comprehensive) systems of social organization; rather, the dimensions attained by capital in their own times were grasped as the promise, the framework, and the precondition for the achievement of some new and more comprehensive socialism. Is this not the case with the yet more global and totalizing space of the new world system, which demands the intervention and elaboration of an internationalism of a radically new type?

II

Terms like "development", "displacement", "identity" and "violence", come together most visibly in the context of the rush for resources that are buried in parts of India inhabited predominantly by "tribals" and the attempt of the state to dispossess by force the tribal population of its lands (which it is doing under the garb of waging war on the "Maoists"). The people living on this land depend upon it for their existence, often completely, sometimes partially. Capitalism and capitalist development, not just in India, but world wide needs these resources to feed the "economy of wants" and so the land has to be taken away. Recently we went to Orissa and spoke to many activists who have been working in areas where dispossession and displacement is being challenged by the local people. In these conversations we found, what we find only too often – the state, using the cover of bringing "development", builds highways to the most underdeveloped parts of the state, which are also the most mineral rich. Mining companies follow, mine for resources, in the process acquiring local land by hook or by crook, and taking from the people the power to reproduce their labor power. This has happened before, in India and in other countries – the "enclosure movement" in 18th century England was the most famous/notorious example of this. Marx had called this process of accumulation of capital through direct dispossession primitive accumulation. This method of accumulation, one must keep in mind, is primitive only when seen in a logical register and historically, as we witness, it can be used by capitalism at any and all points. Michael Perelman writes:

> While primitive accumulation was a necessary step in the initial creation of capitalism, it actually continues to this day. For example, at the time of this writing [Perelman's essay], petroleum and mining companies are displacing indigenous people in Asia, Africa, Latin America and even in the United States. (Saad-Filho, 2003, p. 125)

Pratyush Chandra and Deepankar Basu (2007) in an essay titled "Neoliberalism and Primitive Accumulation in India" argue that primitive accumulation is not simply the originary moment of capitalism but is also constitutive of it. Starting with the premise that the very existence of capitalism is predicated upon its expansion and the continuous separation of laborers from the means of production they argue that while in a perfectly functional capitalist setup the market takes care of this recurrent enactment of the capital-relation, "at the boundaries (both internal and external), where capitalism encounters other modes of production, property and social relations attuned to those modes and also to the earlier stages of capitalism, other ways of subsistence, primitive accumulation comes into play. More often than not, direct use of force is necessary to effect the separation at the boundaries" (Chandra and Basu, 2007).

Neoliberalism is a response to the crisis of the Keynesian welfare state, through a reassertion of the absoluteness of the power of the ruling class and a restructuring of the state as regulator of circulation into a more partisan mould. The state even in its welfarist avatar was an organ of the ruling class, but now it becomes more blatantly than ever a tool in its hands. "Despite the talk of separating the political from the economic, which is a staple rhetoric of the current phase, it is the state as the instrument of politico-legal repression that facilitates neoliberal expansion. Firstly, the state intervenes with all its might to secure control over resources – both natural and human ("new enclosures") – and secondly, to ensure the non-transgression of the political into the economic, which essentially signifies discounting the politics of labor and the dispossessed from affecting the political economy" (Chandra and Basu, 2007). An interesting account of this process is offered in "Aspects of India's Economy", No. 44-46. The relationship between the model of development that the Indian state (now) espouses and impoverishment of the people is explored in great detail, and how development itself becomes exclusion is established.[1]

Of Identities and Co-option

I

Marxian attempts to understand Indian reality, with their "fixation" with "class" and "mode of production" have not found sympathy in Indian sociology. These analyses do not hold, it is argued, because caste is the dominant feature of 'social stratification' in India. This objection is predicated upon the understanding that class, in being an import, even if it has managed to ground itself in India, is only an addition to forms of stratification; caste has its own grounds and class its own. "Overlaps" are acknowledged, but in the same breath comes the warning that class remains a relatively less affective part of this reality; capitalism/class/class-struggle together are said to form one aspect of Indian reality (owing, some many scholars might suggest, to the experience of colonialism), while caste, patriarchy, religion with their own respective baggage form other aspects.

There are two arguments to be made to combat these objections, the first takes issue with their epistemological foundations, and the second with their ahistoricity. Firstly then; the reduction of notions like capitalism and class to ontological fixities (admittedly, something which Marxist scholars have also been guilty of) implicit in these objections does not recognize that it is the logic of capitalist production which is re-enacted in each reality, not its form. India can be capitalist, and just that, even if the Indian reality has a bazillion other features which Europe never had to contend with. Of course, formally speaking, it is a different capitalism. Secondly: Even as the process started by the 'colonial encounter' unfolded, the seeds of capitalism were already coming to fruition in the decaying structures of the Mughal feudal order. Indian reality, of which the caste system and the experience of colonization both were parts, was giving birth to Indian capitalism. Capitalism, as a possibility, was not superimposed upon, or imported into the Indian landscape, but was borne by its own facticity. In an essay entitled, "Potentialities of Capitalistic Development in the Economy of Mughal India," in addition to establishing that the Mughal economy was highly monetized and dominated by domestic industry, Irfan Habib (1995) also shows that contrary to usually held opinion, caste did not obstruct the emergence of capitalism in India.

> It has been held, and the opinion has been powerfully reinforced by Weber, that the caste system put a brake on economic development, through separating education from craft, segregating skills, preventing intercraft mobility, and killing or restricting individual ambition in the artisan...Three or four points ought to be borne in mind. First, the mass of ordinary or unskilled people formed a reserve, from which new classes of skilled professions could be created when the need arose...Secondly, in any region there was often more than one caste following the same profession, so that where the demand for products of a craft expanded, new caste artisans could normally be drawn to that place. More important still, castes were not eternally fixed in their attachment to single professions or skills. Over a long period, economic compulsions could bring about a radical transformation in the occupational basis of caste. (Habib, 1995, pp. 216-217)

Caste was present at, and constitutive of, the foundational moment of Indian capitalism, and is, hence, also a functional characteristic of its being – the last few decades show how Indian capitalism first contained discontent, by limiting its expression to caste-assertions, and then sublimated it through elite formation. It used caste-division to not only resolve contradictions that its inherently self-contradictory nature threw, but also to perpetuate itself.

II

"Country feeds town", has gone from being a catch phrase for "backward-looking" reformers to become a sort of theoretical cliché. In the current Indian conjuncture, however, as a few say often, the cliché has come back to life. That tribes of Chhattisgarh, Jharkhand, Orissa etc. are sitting on mineral resources which are needed for the country's "development" is again a discursive commonplace these days. Many opposed to development at such costs say: "it's their land, their resources; they should be allowed to decide what is to be done with it." The tribal/non-tribal identitarian binary being posed by many anti-displacement assertions is implicit in the first statement concerning country and town. It seems as if it is impossible to talk without creating "identities".

Each utterance, right from the moment of its enunciation contradicts some other – the bad universality of abstract labor does not demolish the particularity of concrete forms of labor, but robs them of their respective singularities. No statement can in its singularity be a universal and coexist with other interests; and the only relation between diverse forms is one of competition. The "I" always defines itself as different from and in opposition to an "other". In this case, ostensibly, the competition is of two, tribal India and non-tribal India. This seems to imply that there are only two groups of interests in India, at least as far as this debate is concerned. As if the people yoked together by these absurd over-generalizations are similar, as if the "tribal community" is completely homogenous, as if the non-tribal community is completely homogenous. The tribal populace wants its lands, the non-tribal wants minerals. We know that calling somebody a non-tribal is hardly calling her/him anything at all; the term is too inclusive to be of use. We also know that there are too many differences of interests as far as the non-tribal population is concerned. In the case of "tribals" this is not so obvious. What is being referred to here is not that there are many different tribes, but that even within each tribe homogeneity is absent; hierarchies and conflicts of interest exist. If in anti-displacement discourses it is held that the tribal people should have the right to decide what happens to their land and resources, one is impelled to ask: if this is allowed, does it guarantee that the resources will be distributed equally? Will those who have never had land, or access to other resources get their share? That this will not happen is easy to see even now. Whenever the question of returning acquired land arises the seemingly homogenous tribal society breaks. Only some owned land earlier. Should the returned land be redistributed? Or should it be returned to those who had owned it earlier? On this question the conflict between the few who owned or own means of production and those who did not/do not becomes clear – what can be called class-conflict becomes apparent.

However, should the struggle of the tribal people for their land be condemned because it does not seem to challenge other forms of exclusion within? Is class somehow a more significant identity than that of being a tribal fighting against dispossession? Many left groups and intellectuals affirm this contention, and draw back from such struggles – "we don't do tribal politics, we do class politics", they say. It is here that we falter in our analysis of politics, and it is in this that the reification of identity is seen. In saying that they do not do "tribal politics", such groups think that they stay safe of the pitfalls of identitarianism, only to create another reified identity – class.

III

> Caste is not merely a division of labor; it is also a division of laborers. (B. R. Ambedkar)
>
> The organization of the proletarians into a class, and consequently into a political party, is continually being upset again by the competition between workers themselves. (Marx and Engels, 1999, p. 98)

The Chashi Mulya Adivasi Sangha was made in the Narayanpatna-Bandhugaon region of the Koraput district of Orissa, by the Adivasis, initially to stop liquor production and the problems caused by its consumption but which eventually led the struggle to get rid of "lemon grass" cultivators. This region is a scheduled tribal area, and as per the Constitution no non-tribal can procure land here. Yet 85%

of the land was owned by non-tribals, who in this instance were Dalit. Huge chunks of land were owned by Dalit landowners, who employed both tribal and non-tribal/Dalit workers to cultivate lemon grass. The Chashi Mulya Adivasi Sangha's struggle against liquor production, partly due to the inertia of its own success and partly because it was a pressing need of the community, had to extend to and change into a struggle against these Dalit landowners. Most Adivasis living in this area are very poor, and migrate to other parts of Orissa for seasonal work. Even those who have some land are only able to reproduce their labor power on what they get from it. The Sangha's struggle transformed into a struggle for land, a struggle which as many point out was completely within the purview of law and the Indian Constitution. This struggle was not driven by an Adivasi "land-hunger". It was simply the struggle to procure the minimum means necessary to reproduce themselves[2], much like the struggle for minimum wages elsewhere.

On this occasion Adivasis, by and large, constituted the exploited and some Dalits owned the means of production. However, there were also a large number of Dalits employed by these landowners. In this struggle against the landowners these Dalits were essentially, as dictated by their location, on the same side as the struggling Adivasis. But they chose to overlook this logical unity of all exploited, to side with the exploiters, deeming their "Dalit" identity more significant. Standing by the Dalit exploiter they stand against their fellow workers. What seems to be a Dalit versus Adivasi struggle is then actually a struggle between two groups of workers, between two segments of the working class.

The first shock: Dalit landowners! This proves that the congealed identity of being a Dalit, of having suffered a "historical wrong" does not make one immune to taking up the role of exploiter. In addition one sees that even among the Dalits there are exploiters and exploited. The Dalit landowner/exploiter in a situation like this cannot be let off because of his Dalit identity. The tribal worker perhaps finds it easy to understand the conflict between her/him and the Dalit-landowner, because of the latter's out-group status. Even though the Dalit-exploiter and the Dalit-worker are not exactly friends, the Dalit-worker continues to side with the Dalit-exploiter. There is more than one reason for this. The first is the exploiter's in-group status. The second, and the most important of all, is the tribal-worker's out-group status, which implies that the tribal-worker is perceived *only* as a competitor in the labor market. The third is the perception of the tribal-worker, that the Dalit-worker is an outsider.

An attempt to resolve this contradiction on a local level has led to the breaking of the Sangha. The Bandhugaon faction has decided to compromise; they will not take land of *all* Dalits, because they say some of them are "poor"[3]. Furthermore they have decided not to put an immediate end to all lemon grass cultivation since it is a source of employment. The Narayanpatna faction tried to take over all the land, end lemon grass cultivation and the ownership of landlords altogether. The thesis and antithesis of a genuine contradiction have been broken apart and the movement has spiraled downwards[4]. The unity needed between the Dalit-worker and the tribal-worker cannot be created here; this conflict cannot be resolved on this level. For these segments of the working class to come together they need to transcend (not *forget*) their identities and allow themselves to be assimilated in the larger struggle against capitalism.

In this localized struggle, a resolution is impossible because local issues are inextricably intertwined with locally defined identities. Only when the immanent logic of transformative politics is generalized, the logic escapes the hold of the local form that pulls it down. In the context of what is happening in Orissa, such a generalization would require this movement to interact with other movements in the state, which are predominantly anti-displacement. Admittedly, unlike the Naryanpatna movement, the moments of enunciation of the other struggles have been defensive, but convergence is necessary and desirable insofar as this union can also benefit these defensive identities, by shifting the grounds on which the battle is being pitched by them, making co-option harder. A programmatic understanding of the situation, evolved gradually through such a dialogic interaction would give the Narayanpatna movement a direction that can be used as a referent to decide upon questions that cannot be answered locally.

IV

The Marxian notion of class is part of a particular act of abstraction performed to understand society and to perceive possibilities of its transformation. Capitalism is understood as a system in which the primary conflict of labor and capital is the dominant determinant of social being. In their analysis of capitalism Marx and Engels came to the conclusion that only those who labor, i.e. workers, have the potential of being agents of radical transformation.

> All previous historical movements were movements of minorities, or in the interest of minorities. The proletarian movement is the self-conscious, independent movement of the immense majority, in the interest of the immense majority. The proletariat, the lowest stratum of our present society, cannot stir, cannot raise itself up, without the whole superincumbent strata of official society being sprung into the air. (Marx and Engels, 1999, p. 100)

"Class struggle" is, in this way, a process of transforming society, and "class" is envisaged not as an identity, like caste or gender or that of being a tribal, but as a process of continuous becoming (conscious) – the working class-in-itself becoming the working class-for-itself.

Where does one find class? It is a problem faced very often by literature students – for instance if one does an analysis of Balzac's *Pere Goriot* keeping in mind the "class angle", how does one go about it. Often critics end up identifying classes with particular characters, and reduce class struggle to an interpersonal battle. The way out of this mess is to study contexts, situations and relationships. One character through the length of a novel does not remain a "member of the working class", although he might well be a factory worker throughout. In life too one finds a factory worker, but not the "working class", and being a factory worker, or just a worker is also an identity. Much like representation in art, representation and self-representation in life needs identities. If one does not identify a worker, one cannot even begin to understand the working class, but to say that being identified as a worker makes a person of the revolutionary class is problematic. A fixed form of the working class to be identified at all times and in all locations does not exist. These indurated forms are identities, which at their moment of articulation express the inherent revolutionary logic of the working class, but are not themselves the complete working class.

The relationship between identities and the process called class is akin to that between particulars and the universal immanent in them, and constructed through continuous abstraction from them; the relationship is dialectical. An identity is valid at a particular spatio-temporal location, and rooted within it is the logic of truly transformative politics. But so long as an identity does not destroy itself, it continuously gets co-opted within the competitive system of capitalism. After a point an identity needs to transcend itself and move towards assimilation into the multitude of struggling identities. At the same time if one does not recognize the struggles of identities, one recognizes nothing, since struggle is necessarily posed in terms of identities. The class-for-itself is always in the process of being constructed, but is never out their, present *a priori,* to be recognized as somehow different from and superior to the multitude of identities.

In the *Communist Manifesto* Marx and Engels repeatedly asserted the significance of the union of many smaller groups of workers waging their local struggles. The struggle for transformation of society is to a large extent the struggle against the divisions within the working class, for it is understood that a united working-class-for-itself would necessarily transform society – in fact society is being transformed in fighting off segmentation within the working class. Marx and Engels wrote:

> Now and then the workers are victorious, but only for a time. The real fruit of their battles lies, not in the immediate result, but in the ever-expanding union of workers. (Marx and Engels, 1999, p. 98)

Only the path that goes through and beyond the thesis and antithesis of identities to a transcendental synthesis can transform the base. It is through identities that articulation and struggle take place, but the struggle of a localized identity is not enough, and is always exposed as superstructural, seen to reinforce the hegemonic structure. Identities are inevitable, and a necessity, but identitarianism divides and restrains the revolutionary multitude. Even in charting out the role of Communists, Marx and Engels had in mind the weeding out of segmentation and sectarianism within the working class, and the creation of a union.

> The Communists are distinguished from the other working-class parties by this only: 1. In the national struggles of the proletarians of the different countries, they point out and bring to the front the common interests of the entire proletariat, independently of all nationality... (Marx and Engels, 1999, p. 102)[5]

Marx and Engels here speak of national struggles, but the essence of what they say deals with insurgent identities in general. A localized identity can only fight for immediate results, after which the struggle and its result is subsumed in the hegemonic system. An identity 'voices' demands, which the system is asked to fulfill. In this two-step act of asking, and being given, the basis of hegemony goes unquestioned; the status of the giver as a giver and his capacity to give goes unchallenged. To put it in other terms (since the state is not itself 'superior' but works on behalf of those who are superior), the state, which in being a state, is a symptom of class power is not questioned. Its role as adjudicator of social relations and as the regulator of value distribution is predicated upon the fact that value is apportioned differentially; at the same time it is its task to maintain and defend the differential apportionment of value. In the act of placing a demand, an identity asks the state for a share of the value being distributed, a share which, presumably, was being denied to it. Once the state allots the identity its share the struggle subsides. This is what one means, when one says that an identity (earlier insurgent) is co-opted into the system.

Challenging Development, Challenging Neoliberal Capitalism

> In 1970...1 per cent of the population had 18 per cent of the wealth, in 1996 the same 1 per cent owned 40 per cent of wealth. After 50 years of independence 26 per cent of the total population lives below the poverty line and 50.56 per cent are illiterate, if we take official figure into account. Even today due to various reasons, 98 children out of every 1,000 between the ages of 1-5, die. An official report of the government's mines and mineral department, published in 1996-97, states that India's natural gas will be consumed within 23 years, crude oil within 15 years, coal within 213 years, copper within 64 years, gold within 47 years, iron ore within 135 years, chromites within 52 years, manganese within 36 years and bauxite within 125 years. All this is taking place in the name of national development. (Debaranjan Sarangi, 'Mining "Development" and MNCs', *EPW* Commentary, April 24, 2004. Quoted in "Factsheet on Operation Green Hunt" published by the 'Campaign against War on People'.)

The notion that growth of manufacturing or services industries is *per se* desirable is a form of fetishism. We need to ask questions such as "Does it create *net* employment (i.e., does it create more jobs than it destroys)?", "Does it meet

> mass consumption requirements (either directly or by developing the capacity to meet these requirements)?", "Does it squander the economic surplus on luxuries? Does it divert resources from more pressing priorities?" "Is it environmentally sustainable? Does it exhaust natural resources?", "Does it uproot people?", and so on. In fact one can cite several industries which, not as an avoidable by-product of their development, but as an essential part of it, harm the masses of people, and benefit only a small class. True, the so-called 'value added' by these industries contributes to the GDP; but this fact merely underlines the irrationality of using GDP as a measure of development. (Aspects of India's Economy, No. 44-46, India's Runaway Growth: Private corporate-led growth and exclusion, p. 9)

It should be clear that changing the manner in which notions like development are envisaged is not an administrative matter. The hegemonic understanding of development is intimately connected to the interests of the hegemonic class, and challenging this development implies challenging hegemony. By extension, to transform the development paradigm would necessarily require the transformation of the power relations structuring a socio-economic formation. Assuming that the need for a unity among those "who have nothing to lose but their chains," is established in our minds, one could contend that the tribal opposition to the form of development that the Indian state has embarked upon, which has emerged in response to the immediate danger to their lives, would need to consciously recognize the constellational unity it bears with workers' opposition to hegemony in other locations. In a paragraph that has already been quoted, Perelman goes on to say:

> Emphasizing the social relations of advanced capitalist production to the exclusion of the ongoing process of primitive accumulation obscures the fact that the struggles of the Ogoni people in Nigeria or the Uwa in Columbia are part of the same struggle as that of exploited workers in Detroit and Manchester. (Saad-Filho, 2003, p. 125)

The same can be said about the "tribals" struggling in Chhattisgarh or Orissa and workers in Gurgaon.[6] As mentioned earlier, displacement and dispossession are forms of primitive accumulation, which is only one form of accumulation of surplus, the other two being relative and absolute surplus value. Capitalist development is about the maximization of the accumulated surplus, and the various forms of accumulation bear an essential unity. If in rural areas we witness this accumulation in the form of direct dispossession, in other locations we see it in the form of increasing alienation of workers from their work, in low wages, increasing work hours, higher and higher degrees of mechanization and lack of job security. If this is the case, then one should also recognize that the challenges being posed to capitalism, at various moments are part of a single struggle to transform society.

Till the conflict between the tribal population and the state continues to be posited in terms of "war", "village community", and so on, this unity of logic will not be recognized – binaries like tribal/non-tribal, village/town etc. will blur the lines along which the actual struggle is being waged and (as was explicated earlier) will give the sense of a false unity of interest between exploited and exploiter. In the moment at which land is acquired the ruling class within the tribal population, which holds most of the land fights back together with the landless tribal who too works on this land. However these landowners usually fight either for compensation or for a part of the new stakes and go over to the state soon enough. In the final analysis the interests of the ruling class within the tribal population and those of "external", more dominant state forms like multinational companies are the same. When the crucial moment of conflict comes this unity between the rulers becomes apparent, the logical unity of parts of the hegemonic structure is clearly reflected in the coordination of forms. To counter this structure, the revolutionary class needs to recognize and consolidate its own multitudinal, insurgent structure. The workers who participated in the huge strikes in the automobile industries in Gurgaon, following the incidents in the Rico factory, are part of the same struggle as the one being waged against dispossession by those tribals who either work on others' land or possess land enough only to reproduce their labor power. To be able to reconfigure the development paradigm, to move to a form of development that takes into account the interests of the majority, the multitudinal majority needs to consciously create itself through the recognition of its diverse and localized forms.

It would be useful here to hint at the difficulties of such a dialectical theorization of the relationship between forms and logic, identities and class. Indeed we find in the difficulty of such a theorization an allegory of the difficulty of class struggle in its entirety. Formally, there is no difference between this understanding of the struggle of an identity (as a moment of class struggle), and the one which reifies the insurgent identity. But logically, there is a difference. The latter gets co-opted at each moment because it fails to question the foreclosure that creates this exploitative structure, seeking to solve, as Laclau (2000) says "a variety of partial problems", while the former posits the struggle of partial forms as the process of creation of a good universality. Formally, the attempt to de-legitimize the struggles of identities, or to "subsume" them, rendering them somehow less important than the struggle against capital, and the attempt to understand how these struggles are moments in the process of struggling against exploitation at large also appear the same. But logically they are different. While the former reifies a partial form of the struggle, and posits it as superior to another, the latter tries to perceive (and create) a constellational unity between these partial forms. Formally there seems no difference between a call to concede the superiority of one identity, and the one to recognize the constellational unity between identities. But logically there is a difference. Totalitarian is the very fabric of capitalist differentiation – on the surface neoliberalism seems to allow difference, but actually it hollows out the concreteness of diverse forms. The unity that we need to forge to end exploitation will have immanent within it the logic of difference, where the universal is the particular and nothing more.

Winding Up

In the era of "late capitalism", with the "death" of the high-capitalist adventurer/entrepreneur, modernism, the individual, of meta-narratives like class and nation, difference rules. On the one hand capitalism is extending its domain, making every "outside" it's part, constantly subsuming the hinterland, repeatedly redefining its own centre, and on the other this is also the era of "identity-assertions". Many have analyzed these phenomena, but the effort to understand them as facets of a systemic totality have been inadequate. Neoliberalism, with its form of decentralized hegemony is able to make use of difference. As capitalism pushes its boundaries, not just geographically, but also in spheres which have been within its geo-political territory without being constitutive of it, identities are posed. Neoliberalism instead of suppressing these is able to co-opt them – it brings identities into competitive relationships, at the same time allowing each validity on its own turf. This horizontality that neoliberalism is able to maintain creates a relativity in values which seemingly makes classical notions like class-struggle, working class, capitalism, communism, transformation, revolution and so on meaningless. If each identity is able to make its assertion, then why talk of fundamental/radical transformation, and furthermore if there are so many equally valid voices how does one decide what the nature of transformation will be? And yet, when encountered by the realities of neoliberalism, the costs of its form of development, one understands the need for transformation. This is the antinomy of postmodernity – one's condition is abominable and because it seems impossible to ascertain the nature of the system, transformation seems unattainable.

This paper, seeking to be an intervention in this situation has tried to hypothesize the possibilities of such a political dialogue between local forms and identities, to take into account the postmodern stress on difference and at the same time assert that a system of differences is a system nonetheless. What is the "internationalism of a radically new type" that Jameson speaks of, but an attempt to rethink the working class as the agent of change within the capitalist system, in the era of postmodernism? To rearticulate the relation between diverse identities and the meta-narrative of the "working class" one can make use of the notion of "class composition", "designed to grasp, without reduction, the divisions and power relationships within and among the diverse populations on which capital seeks to maintain its dominion of work throughout the social factory – understood as including not only the traditional factory but also life outside of it which capital has sought to shape for the reproduction of labor power" (Cleaver, 2003, p. 43). What have been called identities in this paper, can, when speaking of class composition be termed as "sectors of the working class." These "sectors of the working class, through the circulation of their struggles, "recompose the relations among them to increase their ability to rupture the dialectic of capital and to achieve their own ends" (Cleaver, 2003, p. 43). The sort of dialogue needed for this recomposition would need to take the form of a direct, political confrontation, an engagement that would leave nothing unchanged; one's identity and the ideology constituted by ones own experience changes in this encounter, even as the other is made to take into account one's identity. "A double agenda", as Cleaver (2003, pp. 55-56) puts it: "the working out of one's own analysis and the critical exploration of 'neighboring' activities, values and ideas."

> The particular interests of passion cannot therefore be separated from the realization of the universal; for the universal arises out of the particular and determinate and its negation... Particular interests contend with one another, and some are

destroyed in the process. But it is from this very conflict and destruction of particular things that the universal emerges... (Hegel, 1974, p. 89)

Endnotes

1. Interestingly the writers try to extract the notion of "primitive accumulation," in its logical purity and conflate history and logic in a manner rejected in this paper's deployment of the said notion. They write:

   "This giant capture of land and natural resources by the corporate sector is superficially similar to the "primitive (or primary) accumulation" of capital which served as a necessary stage of capitalist development in Europe. It resembles that stage in its brutality and venality. But whereas the capital thus accumulated in the original countries of capitalist development was deployed in manufacturing activity that absorbed the bulk of the dispossessed rural labour force, such absorption is very restricted here." (Aspects of India's Economy, No. 44-46, India's Runaway Growth: Private corporate-led growth and exclusion.)

   The difference between the "original" European situation and the current one in India that they point out is certainly present. But the implicit assertion that the "proletarianized" workforce needs to be absorbed in the location where dispossession occurs lacks logic. The dispossessed do become part of what Marx had called the latent reserve army of labour, and this is "absorption" enough.
2. Pratyush Chandra writes:

   "Now, the sense of being dispossessed is rampant among the rural poor, those who are ready to take up arms. Whatever be their identity, they come mostly under the class of allotment-holding workers, a term that Kautsky and Lenin used to characterise the majority of the so-called "peasantry" – land in whose possession is just for reproduction of their own labour-power. Hence, rural struggles today, including against land acquisition and those led by the Maoists, are not merely against threats to their livelihood but to life itself – to the very sphere of their reproduction." (Chandra, 2009)
3. In situations like these, using a definition of poverty alien to

the context can cause problems. Compared to the urban middle class even the Dalit exploiter is "poor." But in that particular context, they control the labour processes of many others through their control over the means of production. Saying that they should not be treated as "class enemies" only blunts the thrust of transformative politics, which in that location is that those who work should own the land and that only food crops should be grown.

4. The other reason for this spiral downwards has been the uncalled for violence that the state has used against the Narayanpatna movement, killing two Adivasis, injuring many other, and forming a violent "shanti sena" to terrorize the people (till the time this paper was written).
5. To complete the quote: "2. In the various stages of development which the struggle of the working class against the bourgeoisie has to pass through, they always and everywhere represent the interests of the movement as a whole." (Marx and Engels, 1999, p. 102)
6. See http://radicalnotes.com/journal/2010/04/28/developing-unrest-new-struggles-in-miserable-boom-town-gurgaon/

References

Butler. J, Laclau, E. and Slavoj, Z. (2000). *Contingency, Hegemony, Universality: Contemporary Dialogue on the Left*. New York: Verso.

Chandra, P. and Basu, D. (2007). Neoliberalism and Primitive Accumulation in India. [http://www.countercurrents.org/chandra090207.htm (accessed on January 16, 2010)].

Chandra, P. (2009). Revolutionary Movement and the "Spirit of Generalization". [http://radicalnotes.com/journal/2009/11/20/the-revolutionary-movement-in-india-and-the-spirit-of-generalisation. (accessed on January 15, 2010)]

Cleaver, H. (2003). Marxian categories, the crisis of capital, and the constitution of social subjectivity today, in Werner Bonefeld (Ed.), *Revolutionary Writing: Common Sense Essays in Post-Political Politics*. New York: Autonomedia.

Habib, I. (1995). *Essays in Indian History: Towards a Marxist Perspective*. Delhi: Tulika Books.

Hegel, G.W.F. (1975). *Lectures in Philosophy of World History.*

Introduction: Reason in History, trans. H.B. Nisbett. Cambridge: Cambridge University Press.

Jameson, F. (1991). *Postmodernism, Or, the Cultural Logic of Late Capitalism*. Durham: Duke University Press.

Marx, K. and Engels, F. (1999). The Communist Manifesto, in Prakash Karat (Ed.) *A World to Win: Essays on The Communist Manifesto*. New Delhi: LeftWord.

Mukherjee, A. (2002). *Imperialism, Nationalism and the Making of the Indian Capitalist Class, 1920-1947*. New Delhi: Sage.

Negri, H. and Hardt, M. (2004). *Multitude*. New York: Penguin Press.

Perelman, M. (2003). The History of Capitalism. In Alfredo Saad-Filho (Ed.) *Anti-Capitalism: A Marxist Introduction*. London: Pluto.

3

"No Rehabilitation" is Ecocide and Genocide: Is There Possibility of Hope?

Savyasaachi

Ecocide and genocide are attributes of labor embedded in its teleology that originates in the Industrial Revolution, underlies all its regimes, and is not an externality. This is now well established by historical experience across the world. To extract resources from nature, at a rate that exceeds many a times the rate at which nature can recuperate and rehabilitate itself is ecocide. This cannot be done without displacing a mass of people and depriving them of conditions for meaningful labor, by means of which they could belong to meaningful human social structures. In this process their capacity to recuperate and rehabilitate themselves is destroyed beyond repair in both nature and human beings.

To displace and not to rehabilitate is ecocide and genocide.

This labor teleology posits a notion of justice, which is inclusive of the elements of equality, freedom and fraternity. These, according to this teleology, are not found in the state of nature; in fact "in nature" these elements are undermined. A necessary "pulling out" of human beings from the state of nature is thus required. In the process of "pulling out" human beings from the state of nature, labor pulls itself out of nature as well. This has devastated and splintered human structures, nature and ecology. Historical experience has shown that the "pulling out of the state of nature" in fact, displaces the critical elements of ethics, culture and aesthetics from their foundational position in human structures, ideas and institutions. A notion of justice devoid of its foundational critical elements is civilizational collapse.

Why is rehabilitation an externality?

Rehabilitation presupposes a sense of belonging. Having pulled itself out of "nature" this sense becomes an externality to the teleology of labor – this is borne out by the fact that it regards the ethical, cultural and aesthetic elements that build the foundations of belonging to be externalities. In the course of "pulling out human beings from the state of nature" it "pulls out" these foundational elements to destroy the notion of belonging itself. For this reason labor teleology belongs "nowhere", and thus the notion of rehabilitation is alien to it.

The human structures of signification are the foundation of a sense of belonging. The relation between the signifier and signified is given in the ethical, cultural and aesthetic norms of a society. When these elements are pulled out and displaced from their critical (foundational) position in the social structures of significations, the relation between the signifier image (of the material world) and the signified concept collapses.

The state and the market, separately until 1989 and together thereafter, have pulled out the foundational elements to promote this "labor teleology." This has strengthened the paradigm of labor that has been destroying the foundational elements of human structures of significations across the globe for over one hundred years. This paradigm is incapable of self-correction and self-improvement.

Since labor teleology belongs "nowhere" it ensures its own reproduction by ensuring the reproduction of capital (which also belongs "nowhere"). For this it pulls out foundational elements to cut delays, increase speed and encourage competition and production of goods and services. In recent history this has been done by creating economic zones, hubs, corridors and mergers. Each impacts a human structure of signification.

Global Zones Dislodging the Local

The process of economic zoning misaligns and destroys lines of articulation between the local and the global. Disastrous climate change, industrial breakdown, the rapidity with which difference degenerates into conflict, conflict turns violent and violence takes the form of war and terrorism, declining immunity and resilience – all of these demonstrate the preceding statement.

Special Economic Zones are created by forcefully removing "nature workers" from natural landscapes – from their foundational structural positions in the order of things in the world – where they work and to which they belong. They are displaced to "nowhere". This dislodgement is eco-genocide. It converts the natural landscape into a battleground where elements of nature are displaced from their foundational structural position. This ecocide pushes diverse nature workers – forest workers, river and ocean people, mountain people, desert people into another battleground in agrarian and industrial economies, where they become part of the reserve army of labor, to take up arms against capital.

Frequent transnational *dislodgment* is necessary to generate development, capital, skilled professionals, unskilled labor, technology and raw materials. The speed of the movement is equally important because it determines directly the rate of production and reproduction, the cost of production and prices. In its absence, various components of the production process cannot be coordinated and synchronized into an efficient system. This is the underlying rationale of the neoliberal "opening up" of the economy. By this is meant that the social, cultural and political boundaries become porous, permeable, and renegotiable. To facilitate this it is necessary that an authoritarian mode of governance be developed alongside.

The violence generated by the battles over natural landscapes displaces people's worldview and ideologically compels them to adopt the "consumerist" way of life.

Hubs misaligning the individual and the collective

Hubs distance, misalign and introduce a parallax in the individual-collective relation. They ensure that goods and services are made available in many places simultaneously, across phenomenal distances in time and space. This introduces *distance* between different aspects of the production process.

What is the significance of this distance?

It makes organizing protest difficult.

This clears the way to put in place mechanisms to reduce the time lag between the introduction of a product or a service in one place and its adoption in other places, especially with respect to technologies. For this reason products based on fresh technologies can be designed with the whole world in mind. New technologies can create their own infrastructure, the same everywhere. For instance, with the black-and-white television there was a twelve years gap for full penetration into the United States and equal penetration in Europe and Japan. In other words, as the technological differential across the globe gets eliminated production will be standardized, leading to manufacture of similar goods everywhere. The reduction of time lag in the diffusion of technology is expected to reduce differences in the quality of production.

This violence percolates to become part of the everyday life of people. The social structures of nature workers crumble and they become part of a society which is crumbling on account of race, class and gender inequalities.

Bypassing conventions

Corridors have been constructed to bypass the conventions of interdependence between part and the whole which is the basis structures of human signification.

Corridors are *by-passes,* the numerous alternate routes to reach and serve customers. These are specialized pathways for unobstructed transfer. For instance, the rise of worldwide, overnight packet delivery services by-passes government postal service. So do fax machines. Some electronic funds transfer bypasses central banks. Other examples of by-pass are multiple T.V. channels, the cable system network and so on. Entrepreneurs change the nature of industries by-passing funding or by creating new routes outside established channels. In the field of conservation corridors are being constructed for protection of specific species, for instance elephant corridors. This contributes to speed by creating unobstructed passage for goods, services and capital, but not for the people at large.

All this by-passes several layers of human social structures and sites of social interaction that mediate between the producer and the consumer. The result is social paralysis – productive capacities degenerate, the vitality of human metabolism is deprived of creative impulse and the collective dissolves into amnesia.

Merging the public and the private

Corporate mergers have created the illusion that the private is the public and vice versa in all fields of social activity and at all levels of social life. This has depleted the buffers between different fields and sectors of social life, exposing them, unprotected against radiations from mega-monopolies. This radiation unleashes a chain reaction compelling all social to clone its image. This cloning constructs multiples of the "one" – the mega-monopoly. This is *multiculturalism.* For instance within countries, giant companies that enjoyed the status of favorites and which were protected as champions of the nation, especially government owned companies, are being merged and opened to competition.

This increasingly leaves no room – time or space – for plural production paradigms to exist and evolve. Crafts, home-based work and self-employing enterprises, gardening, shifting cultivations and multi-crop cultivations are destroyed. Corporate monopolies "monopolize" the definition of work, nature and productivity and also the relations that comprise these. Consequently, worldviews are displaced and obliterated. What remains is a viewpoint to specific issues. Does not capital generate, in this way, monopolies, pushing people into reservations by means of "affirmative action", displacing them from their own cultural ways of life? It may be worthwhile to consider how "affirmative action" could be contributing to the making of an exclusivist identity. So long as monopolies continue to generate scarcity, conflicts over reservations and affirmative action will continue.

As was said earlier labor teleology displaces people into "nowhere". What does this look like?

The four attributes of labor teleology – dislodging, misaligning, by-passing and by merging – have taken away from production in general, its foundational elements (ethics, aesthetics and culture) with great speed. In the absence of these elements all spaces in villages, towns and cities are virtually being made into global villages. As the world is global, capital spreads to make it a global village, all village localities under pressure to clone and displace into this imaginary virtual space.

The world, it is said, is becoming a virtual, global village; people are being displaced from existing villages and these villages are being destroyed. Dish antennas, high rise buildings, shopping malls are now spreading like viruses. Progressively, it is becoming difficult to differentiate between people belonging to different cultures from the way they dress, the food they eat, the books they read, the modes of transportation they use, or by looking at their patterns of entertainment. In short, a person is likely to find similar things in any part of the world.

Europeans can find in India, food, shelter and clothing of their taste, even as Indians can find what is tasteful to them in Europe. People from different cultures expect that over the next decade all aspects of life will be standardized and accessible to everyone. For instance, in a shopping mall it is possible to eat from cuisines from different parts of the world. Will this make it possible that no visitor feel a stranger in a foreign land? The difference between the local and the global is expected to dissolve!

Several destinations can be reached with by-passes, flyovers that take one across crossroads, in a state of perpetual motion, without feeling the need to slow down, or become part of the crowd, or exchange a smile or a scorn.

Though the thrill of speed is fascinating, it releases energy for short durations and in spurts. Not everyone has the capacity to cope with it. It takes its toll on the human body, the spiritual self and on social relations. When one peeps inside the life of people, one discovers there, more pain that they have to cope with than they are prepared for. Today, war is a spectacle a person can view in the privacy of the bedroom or in the company of friends and visitors in the living room.

When a person steps out into the open, leaving these private fascinations, the hot sun scorches the skin and tires the soul, pushing it back quickly into the comfort of enclosed, air-conditioned spaces. Indeed, there has grown an attraction for fair skins that can tan and look sexy and seductive. Slowly, pictures in advertisements and aspects of real life are becoming similar. In fact, images on the screen and those found in real life, increasingly, seem to mirror each other.

Consumerism, cloning and seduction are three aspects of identity formation in the global world – to be able to masturbate and feel the sensations of love, keeping the skin from wrinkling and enjoying a sense of perpetual youthfulness. It takes away romance from life. It deprives being in the world of the seasoning of the summer heat, the cool monsoon, the warm, winter sun, and the sweat and blood of hard work, leaving a person vulnerable. This leaves space open to the "acquired immunity syndrome". The opulent virtual reality of the global village leaves people in a state of confusion, ill-equipped to make sense of their schizophrenic lives.

The economic urgency of producing ever more "novel-seeming" goods (from clothing to airplanes), at ever increasing rates of turnover, is the internal and super-structural expression of a whole new wave of military and economic domination throughout the world. In its most active mode, this labor teleology lays down mores for torture, death and terror.

A cumulative effect of dislodging, misaligning, bypassing and merging is the displacement of responsibility for devastation and splintering on to the "third world" – for instance, the location of polluting industries in the "third world," or the global south.

In the discussion so far ecocide and genocide has been conceptualized as the collapse of human structures of significations. Furthermore, it is being contended that ecocide and genocide are embedded in the teleology of industrial labor and for this reason rehabilitation is an externality to this teleology.

Is there no hope?

Radical Insistence and Hope in the Face of Civilizational Collapse

What is it to have no home, no belonging and no meaning to existence? Labor teleology set its first imprint on the lives of the indigenous people of North America. It is now common knowledge that the possibility of the coming into being of the United States of America was created by the cultural genocide of the Indians. The first few generations of White migrants destroyed, by design, the ways in which the Indian people lived. Those who survived were displaced into reservations, without rehabilitation.

How did the indigenous people respond to the impossibility of continuing to live their way of life? Jonathan Lear's *Radical Hope-Ethics in the Face of Devastation* attempts to describe the response of the Crow people. In September 1886, the Sioux chief, Sitting Bull, who had been a formidable enemy of the US government made a visit to the Crow reservation. He stayed for two weeks. Here were two traditional enemies – who had slaughtered each other in recurrent waves for over a century coming together to talk things over in the wake of radical historical change (Lear, 2006, pp. 106-107). This was an extraordinary meeting.

From the perspective of Sitting Bull, Plenty Coups (the Crow chief), was a "gullible sap or worse, a collaborator with malign forces" (Lear, 2006, p. 107), "a fool [who] would cooperate with the white man" (Lear, 2006, p. 148). "To do so would be to surrender one's personal authority and sacrifice one's followers to the whims of petty officials" (Lear, 2006, p. 106).

According to Lear's account Plenty Coup brought together other Crow chiefs to form a united front in negotiating with the US government. "He actively encouraged young Crow to acquire white man's education..." (Lear, 2006, pp. 4-5).

> He idealized neither the white man nor his tribe...The white man often promises to do one thing and then, when [he] acted at all, did another. He is someone who fools nobody but himself...He was no easier on his tribe...You who once were brave have turned into pigs. I am ashamed of you. Self-pity has stolen your courage, robed you of your spirit and self-respect. Stop mourning the old days; they are gone with the buffalo... (Lear, 2006, pp. 139-140)

Was Sitting Bull correct in his judgment of Plenty Coups? Lear advocates Plenty Coup's vision as opposed to Sitting Bull's.

> To promote that position, one would need to argue that even in such extreme circumstances certain forms of human excellence are still possible. Rather than arguing for radical hope in isolation, one would argue that such hope plays a crucial role in a courageous life. Thus we are led into an

> investigation of what courage might be in such challenging times. If we can persuade ourselves that even in these extreme circumstances courage is a genuine virtue – that is, a state of character whose exercise contributes to the living of an excellent life – then if we can also show that radical hope is an important ingredient of such courage, we have thereby provided a legitimacy of such hope. (Lear, 2006, p. 107)

Lear goes on,

> I would like to consider hope as it might arise at one of the limits of human existence...Radical hope anticipates a good for which those who have the hope as yet lack the appropriate concepts with which to understand it...In the light of this understanding he suggests that Plenty Coups responded to the collapse of his civilization with radical hope. (Lear, 2006, p. 103)

A brief description of the historical context follows.

According to Lear, the Crow were a nomadic, hunting, warrior tribe. They settled, around 1700, in what is now Montana and Wyoming. Their way of life was hunting and warring. Their rivals were the Sioux, the Black-feet and the Cheyenne. Their way of life was a continuous insistence, on account of nomadic movement, on their territorial boundaries "to exert proprietary claim over the animals (horses and buffaloes) within its shifting domain; and it need[ed] to repulse proprietary claims of their rivals. Counting coups is the minimal act that forces recognition of these boundaries *from the other side*". (Lear, 2006, p. 18)

The act of counting coups entailed "hitting one's enemy with a coup-stick *before* harming him" (Lear, 2006, p. 16). All clans within a tribe had their respective coup-stick. It was an established practice that "if in a battle a warrior stuck his coup stick in the ground, he must not retreat or leave the stick...The planting of a coup-stick was symbolic of the planting of a tree that could not be felled". (Lear, 2006, p. 13)

In the Crow cultural system a sense of shame is at the core of courage and bravery.

> "A courageous person, for example, will not only have good judgment about what counts as a shameful act; he will rule out such acts as possible (for him). If one has been brought up say, in the pattern of Crow excellence, one will likely have an internalized shame-mechanism that reflects the Crow understanding of courage." (Lear, 2006, p. 63)

The processes leading to a civilizational collapse began when the Crow willingly moved onto the reservation. The type of devastation the Crow actually endured "was of a different order from anything for which they could have thoughtfully planned" (Lear, 2006, p. 24). Under "conditions of confinement and poor sanitation in the reservation they lost the ability to resist disease and the younger generation was all but wiped out" (Lear, 2006, p. 27).

Around the 1840's because "buffaloes were disappearing from the traditional Sioux grounds they were pressured to move to the Crow" (Lear, 2006, p. 73). On account of terrible military pressure from the migration of the Sioux, the hunting ground dominated by the Crow was "reduced to neutral ground...The once formidable Crow were a much weakened people...The era of vague borders and friendly mountains was over. In this situation in the 1850's to be without guns, blankets and ammunition was tantamount to suicide." (Lear, 2006, pp. 22-23)

Against this unrelenting pressure from the Sioux the Crow signed the Fort Laramie Treaty in 1851 (Lear, 2006, p. 26). The 1860s were a period of terrible war with the Sioux and in 1867 a second Fort Laramie Treaty was signed with the USA. During this period, the Crow fought on the side of the USA, against their common enemy, the Sioux. "Crow land was reduced to 2 million acres". (Lear, 2006, p. 26) "Hunting became impossible...because the Crow were forbidden to pursue a nomadic life...The younger generation was wiped out..." (Lear, 2006, p. 27)

This was the period in which Plenty Coup grew up. Pushing the limits of understanding was a Crow cultural practice. The Crow encouraged the young to go off into nature and dream. In 1855-56, when he was nine years of age, he was "called to go off and dream". "He went to a mountaintop. On the first night he had no dream, so he chopped off a piece of his finger to encourage a vision. Such behavior was not unusual." (Lear, 2006, p. 66) According to Plenty Coup, after chopping the piece of his finger off he saw

> "...four war eagles sitting in a row along a trail of blood just above me. But they did not speak to me, offered nothing at all. But from other accounts it seems that Plenty Coups was actually visited by the golden eagle, who offered him his powers....It is known that he had the lifelong assistance of golden eagle and that his powers allowed him to succeed as a warrior and war leader" (Lear, 2006, pp. 90-91).

"On the second night in the wilderness, young Plenty Coup had his dream." (Lear, 2006, p. 69) Dreaming was an act of courage. What did the dream say?

In the dream Plenty Coup is taken to see a very old and feeble man sitting in the shade of a particular tree. He is told that this old man is Plenty Coup himself. Furthermore, in the dream there is a tremendous storm in which the Four Winds begin a war against the forest. All trees are knocked over, except one (Lear, 2006, p. 70). A voice told Plenty Coup that a Chickadee person lodges in this tree. He is a good listener and is willing to work for wisdom.

> Whenever others are talking together of their success and failure, there you will find the Chickadee person listening to their words. But in all his listening he does his own business. He never intrudes, never speaks in strange company, and yet never misses a chance to learn from others. He gains success and avoids failure by learning how others succeeded or failed...Develop your body, but do not neglect your mind, Plenty-Coups. It is the mind that leads a man to power, not strength of the body. (Lear, 2006, pp. 70-71)

At the time when Plenty Coup saw this dream the Crow had reason for concern, for the buffalo were disappearing from the traditional Sioux grounds, and as a result the Sioux were pressured to move into Crow territory.

Lear points, out that in the 1920s, the US government "decided to destroy all the so-called wild horses on the western plains, in response to complaints from white farmers. These included horses roaming on the Crow reservation that the tribe considered their own. This was against the wishes of the tribe, and caused much pain." (Lear, 2006, p. 58)

Lear tries to understand three issues in terms of the language of the Crow: is this confrontation with the white man a civilizational collapse for the Crow? Of what significance is the dream, in addition to being a way of accessing that, which is inaccessible to the intellect? In what way was Plenty Coups' response better than that of Sitting Bull?

With respect to the first question Lear asks what could Plenty Coup's have meant when he said "After this nothing happened" (Lear 2006, p. 2). It seems to be a declaration of a moment when history came to an end. But what could it mean for history to come to exhaust itself? (Lear, 2006, p. 3) Lear suggests that a way of life is vulnerable in various ways, on account of its own culture and in relation to external forces. People as participants in that way of life inherit vulnerability. What would it be to be a witness to this breakdown? (Lear, 2006, p. 6)

> What is the possibility of things ceasing to happen... [and]...how ought we to live with it? So: it is one thing to give an account of the circumstances in which a way of life actually collapses; it is another to give an account of *what it would be* for it to collapse. And it is yet another to ask: How ought we to live with the possibility of collapse? ... We are trying to grasp an extreme possibility of human existence – in part so that we can grasp the scope and limits of human possibility. (Lear, 2006, pp. 9-10)

The expression "nothing happened" draws attention to the extreme possibilities of human existence and also to the limits and scope of human possibility at a moment when a way of life has to confront exhaustion – a crisis of stamina. Here it becomes possible to understand that that the limit and scope of human possibility is embedded in 'cultural reserves'. According to Lear the Crow did not understand a *gamble with necessity*. "This is a gamble that the entire field of possibilities will remain stable; that one will continue to be able to judge success and failure in its terms." (Lear, 2006, p. 26)

Lear draws attention to the amazing cultural reserve that is embedded in the notions of shame and courage.

This story of Sitting Bull and Plenty Coup shows "the tolerance of a space of competing meanings that itself came under attack at the end of the nineteenth century" (Lear, 2006, p. 30). For instance, in relation to other tribes, in their Crow-like way they insisted upon the reality of Crow life – even the enemy had to accept this reality. And the Crow life had a reality because it could be insisted upon (Lear, 2006, p. 34).

Plenty Coups was pushed into a situation where this space was not available; the terms of reference of this culture were being lost and the way of life had became unlivable; the categories of his life had become uninhabitable. The categories that were being made available by force were not adequate to tell his story. And these were the circumstances in which he was called upon to act. The transition to the reservations destroyed the ground for cultural value attached to pride, courage and bravery that gave practical, everyday life direction of purpose. Cultural questions central to the Crow way of life lost meaning.

Is it possible for people to continue to act practically without the rich framework in which such acts gain meaning? This framework and the sense is a source of pride, embedded in the conception of a good life. The paradigmatic virtue for good life was courage, understood in terms of a nomadic way of life and a warring culture – bravery in hunting and in battle. It was no longer fitting and meaningful to have horses or to win a battle or to hunt. In the face of a collapse what is the way to get meaning back into life and stop living a life which one does not understand?

In confinement in the reservation, the Crow, according to Lear, were confronted with a stark choice: "either they had to give up an idea that there was any longer a courageous way to live, or they had to alter their conception of what courage was" (Lear, 2006, p. 64).These moments can enrich or destroy a culture. Language and individual psychologies are strained to respond to the absolute-unprecedented – namely the impossibility of continuing to be what one is.

Was there a certain possibility deeply embedded in a culture's thick conception of courage? That is, were there ways in the culture's traditional understanding of courage that could draw upon inner resources to broaden the understanding of what courage might be? This would entail drawing on their tradition in novel ways in the face of novel challenges. What conditions would make it possible?

Lear tells us of Plenty Coup's extraordinary, fitting, and courageous act which looked this collapse straight in the eye. "At Tomb of the Unknown Soldier he ceremonially laid down his coup-stick." (Lear, 2006, p. 60) This act showed that "there was still room in the radically altered circumstances to think about what it was appropriate to do...It was appropriate to express the demise of the traditional understanding of the appropriate." (Lear, 2006, p. 60)

How is this act extraordinary and not one of surrender? What went into the act of laying down the coup-stick? To the outsider this act can look like surrender. Lear tries to perceive the meaning of this act from within the framework of the Crow way of life and culture. It was an act of courage for "courage requires that one be able to regulate a sense of honor and shame – standards of which were rooted in traditional community values" (Lear, 2006, p. 84). Plenty Coups had learnt that this sense of self-regulation was the core of being courageous.

Lear emphasizes that it is important to recognize that when a civilization collapses, there are likely to be types of acts which if performed in the old world would have been shameful but in radically new circumstances ought not to count as shameful. This requires a transformation of the framework that determines ones experiences of shame, so that one does lose sight of what constitutes a shameful act and what does not (Lear, 2006, pp. 88-89). Lear infers that "precisely because Plenty Coups sees that a traditional way of life is coming to an end, he is in a position to embrace a peculiar form of hopefulness. It is basically the hope for revival: for coming back to life that is not yet intelligible". (Lear, 2006, p. 95)

This brings us to the second question; in such a situation what was the significance of the dream? As it was pointed out earlier, in the Crow understanding dreaming is an act courage that pushes beyond what is intelligible to the conscious mind.

According to Yellow Bear, the wisest man, the dream said that the white man will take and hold the country. Furthermore, by listening as "the Chickadee-person listens" they may escape this and keep their lands (Lear, 2006, p. 72).

The dream recommended, in the face of collapse, listening "like a Chickadee-person", with the power of the golden eagle. The Crow took their dreams to reveal an order of the universe that was typically hidden from ordinary conscious life. Dreams were often used by the tribe to not only predict a future event; but also "to struggle with the intelligibility of events that lay at the horizon of their ability to understand" (Lear 2006, p. 68).

The dream pointed to the challenge they had to face. "They explicitly recognized in an official council that their buffalo-hunting way of life was coming to an end, and they decided to ally with the white man against their enemies." (Lear, 2006, p. 73) With the horses gone the Crow culture was damaged deeply. This was traumatic and tragic for a proud tribe for which the horse was of great importance.

The dream was more than an imaginative response to an impending disaster. It was one of those capacities of the imagination that constitutes a courageous soul. The radical hope that Plenty Coups' dream generated was a manifestation of imaginative excellence embodied in the ideal of the Chickadee-person, the capacity to listen. His commitment to the dream was more than an instance of his specific religious obligations. The dream gave him an insight which allowed him to hold onto the core of commitment at the time of collapse. "His dream became the thread through which he could lead his people through radical discontinuity." (Lear, 2006, p. 148)

> Through his dream – and his fidelity to it – Plenty Coups was able to transform the destruction of a telos into a teleological suspension of the ethical. (Lear, 2006, p. 146)

There can be various ways of looking at this. Plenty Coups' act of listening (and not fidelity) to the dream was possible only if his mode of being in the world was for its own sake. The Crow culture, as described by Lear, had no notion of telos, and this was its strength. The white man brought a telos that displaced the Crow into reservations. Plenty Coups' insistence was to not give in to the white man's telos.

This brings us to the third question: Was Plenty Coups' response better than Fighting Bull's and for what reasons? Other than courage, what aspects of the dream equipped Plenty Coups to face a historically unprecedented and catastrophic situation? This pertains to the teleological suspension of the ethical. What did the signing of the treaty get for the Crow?

The dream calls one to not lose hope even when there is no way to grasp an absolutely unprecedented situation, to hold on to the notion of "good" even when everything one experiences is to the contrary "for no reason at all". This is radical hope. Its basis is nothing other than itself. This is not blind faith in the face of a "no possibilities situation", and neither is it mere optimism, which refers to the hope of realizing ones wishes (Lear, 2006, pp. 112-116). On the contrary, it is an exercise of good judgment: firstly, reality is ungraspable (Lear, 2006, p. 113); secondly, the recognition that goodness could be beyond our grasp – the goodness of the world is beyond our finite powers (Lear, 2006, p. 121); thirdly, the dream-space is one of possibilities (Lear, 2006, p. 133); fourthly, the ideal of Chickadee is suggestive of a method to deal with a catastrophic situation – to listen carefully and not be in haste to act, and to learn from others; fifthly, this is a robust acceptance, a coming to terms with the finitude of the human condition, without which the realm of possibilities is inaccessible; and finally, this is grounded in the view that in such a situation it would be shameful "to turn ones back on the genuine wisdom of others" (Lear, 2006, p. 145).

This recognition of human limits even as it is recognition of vulnerability on the one hand it provides courage to take risks on the other (Lear, 2006, p. 120). The risk that Plenty Coups was taking was "not in the traditional paradigm, namely of death in the battlefield. It was a greater risk: that one had reoriented oneself towards shame in the wrong sort of way, and was unwittingly doing something shameful, not fine, that one's strategy would not ultimately work and that the Crow would lose their land, their values – indeed that they would be destroyed as a people." (Lear, 2006, p. 146)

The signing of the treaty, in this perspective, was a very high risk. To what extent did this pull the Crow out of this situation of collapse?

Plenty Coups was not able to avoid the allocation of reservation land. However the Crow were able to negotiate with significant success. They retained all mineral rights (Lear, 2006, p. 138); they were able to keep their mountains (Lear, 2006, p.139); the possibility that the tribe might be able to buy back the land sold by members to white farmers was discussed (Lear, 2006, p. 139).

Keeping in mind Sitting Bull's criticism of Plenty Coups we need to enquire how he responded to the historic situation.

In 1889, throughout the Sioux reservations there was much talk of the coming of a new messiah who would save the Indians. In the following year (1891) he would wipe out all whites in a catastrophe. This took hold of Sitting Bull. At "Standing Rock" participants danced until they dropped from exhaustion. They abandoned all activity to bring about this cataclysm. When officers came to arrest Kicking Bear who had introduced the dance, Sitting Bull promised that Kicking Bear would go back to his reservation, but that the Ghost Dance would continue. The dance continued through October to December, when it was forcibly ended on December 15, 1890, when the tribal police tried to arrest Sitting Bull on orders of the Indian agent; he was killed by the police in the midst of a violent outbreak (Lear, 2006, pp. 149-150).

Plenty Coups opposed the messianic religion. (Lear, 2006, p. 50)

The Crisis – Being without Belonging

We can now turn our gaze to the absolutely unprecedented finality of industrial labor teleology manifest in "displacements and no rehabilitation" in contemporary time. Is there a clash of civilizations? The indigenous populations across the world are struggling against the new ways of taking away land. Colonizers continue to leave no space for the indigenous people. They continue to undermine, systematically, the peoples' material and spiritual ground.

There are two kinds of responses - those who follow the line taken by Plenty Coups and those who follow the line taken by Sitting Bull. The intentions and reasons behind these lines are different. We need to ask what these differences are.

The questions Plenty Coups and Sitting Bull faced continue – are there possibilities other than that of either annihilating one's own self or becoming what one is not, by engaging in a battle unto death, for which one is ill-equipped and which one is thus bound to lose.

As history shows labor teleology continues this attack even today. It seeks to ensure that insistence fails, making it an unintelligible act. This Lear suggests is the same as the "breakdown of that in terms of which happening occurs" (Lear, 2006, p. 38).

This is not the same as identity crisis. It is much more. The state and the market are now the left and the right profiles of corporate capital. Today, in India, labor teleology pushes people to this "no rehabilitation collapse" in at least three ways. First, by physically pushing people out; second, by letting them be where they are but taking away their structures of significations and finally by forcefully making their homes into battle grounds. The first is the way of the political Right, the second is the way of the political Centre and the third is the way of the political Left. This suggests that the ideological/theoretical differences and alignments have been dislodged, by-passed and merged.

The teleology underlying Marxian dialectical materialism, as we know it today and neoliberalism compels them, for different reasons, to use arms and abet the armament industry and all that makes it a necessity. This absence of any difference between the Left, Center and Right comes along with the alliance between the state and the market.

Displacement without rehabilitation is "being without belonging" at all levels of social existence. When people are displaced from fertile lands to find space for building missile stations, humongous dams for generation of hydroelectricity, multiple lane highways, and so on, do not those few who are beneficiaries, also acquire a being without belonging?

From the standpoint of Sioux chief Plenty Coup, each of these is an aspect of civilizational dynamics. Insistence is freed from the labor teleology in the face of civilizational collapse. It insists on the necessity to explore a sense of hope in "that which is not labor teleology".

Reference

Lear, J. (2006). *Radical Hope: Ethics in the face Devastation*. Cambridge, Massachusetts: Harvard University Press.

4

Ventilating Predicament of Development: New Economic Enclaves and Structural Violence in India

Manisha Tripathy Pandey

> Force is the midwife of every old society which is pregnant with a new one. It is itself an economic power.
>
> *Karl Marx, Capital*

Any form of exercise of power is violent if people's views and actions are ignored, repressed and restricted without consent. There are two ways of thinking about violence: in terms of an intentional act of excessive or destructive force, or in terms of a violation of rights (Bufacchi, 2005). Violence is intrinsic to the human condition or social structure although it is always mediated through human agency. The relationship between violence and the economic world orders at different historical junctures have been analyzed by various theorists: violence and feudalism by Hegel (1977), violence and capitalism by Marx (1976) and Engels (1987), and violence and imperialism by Fanon (1966). All of them encapsulate the dialectical nature of historical revolutions of their times. Now, the structural violence of global capitalism has penetrated into the developing world, leading to exploitation of the poor and of natives.

The sufferings of those who are poor and remote, in terms

of both economy and culture, are aggravated by the setting up of new economic enclaves in India called the Special Economic Zones (SEZs). The actual effect of this developmental project is increase in exploitation of the weak by the rich, of the underdeveloped inside by the developed world outside and structural violence. Structural violence is the combination of extreme inequality, social exclusion and humiliation, or assault on people's dignity (Uvin, 1999). This essay uses the theory of structural violence to illuminate how structural inequalities systematically deny some people their basic human needs. Using Galtung's (1969, 1990) notion of structural violence, this essay tries to understand structural violence as a concrete social phenomenon, as illustrated by the setting up of SEZs in India, which leads to exploitation and inequality. Exerted at the structural level and not simply at the level of human agency, violence may be regarded as present whenever a person's potential and capacity to lead a full life is inhibited.

In the contemporary world, a number of ambiguities and paradoxes are associated with the notion of development. This essay is an effort to understand the dilemma of development-induced displacement, the question of rehabilitation, resettlement and the consequences thereof, especially for the vulnerable groups – all these are manifestations of structural violence. It is the development policy of the Indian State, the widening levels of disparity and the continuing problems of social deprivation and structural violence when compounded with the effort to restrict access to "common property resources" that give rise to social anger, desperation and unrest. In almost all cases the affected people try to ventilate their grievances using peaceful, or at times violent means of protest; they take out processions, sit on demonstrations, and submit petitions. Thus structural violence leads to agential violence or violent conduct.

Any development project is brutal, ruthless and violent if it does not take the people as its point of departure and active participants. Development projects such as dams, industrialization, mining, and other mega-infrastructural projects like SEZs cause upheaval and displacement of communities. The Special Economic Zones are the latest to join the bandwagon of economy-driven development. Large piece of lands are acquired by business tycoons to develop business or industrial cities. The lands are acquired by the state at low costs with promises of giving jobs and other benefits, and are then sold to these companies at huge profits. The companies then forcefully evict the landowners and most of them become laborers in the new industry. The establishment of SEZs on agricultural land leads to the conversion of a peasant into a proletariat. The new proletariat finds it difficult to confront and cope with machine-based technology and is unable to participate in the industrial life in which handicraft or agricultural skills are altogether undermined. This phenomenon poses large questions and threats to the very social and cultural existence of the people affected. This essay is focused on the larger issues involved in SEZs, on their social impact and that on individual welfare, and on how structures of property and power cause violence.

All forms of socio-economic development involve choices, explicit or implicit, about priorities – to reduce pain, suffering and violence or focus upon other objectives such as economic growth and the associated benefit of some *vis-à-vis* others. The setting up of SEZs is being questioned and this is an attempt to open up the debates. The question is about whether violence is integral or accidental in this kind of a developmental path. Is violence only a temporary part of a transitory phase of restructuring or is it a permanent structural feature of neoliberal times? The creation of a free-trade zone also brings with it a claustrophobic situation for people as the core values of "well-being" are pushed away. The generation of this claustrophobia leads to pain and suffering. The establishment of SEZs damages something that people value. It is important to ventilate the paradoxes and the developmental dilemma of these new economic enclaves, which this essay explores.

Understanding Structural Violence

Structuralism and structural violence present a picture of a vastly unequal world. Structural violence is embedded in the current world system. This form of violence is centered on apparently inequitable social arrangements. To understand structural violence, one must first take a structuralist view of the world, where structures and institutions are central to analysis. Structuralist analysis focuses on the holistic aspects of society, including interdependent relationships among individuals, collectivities, institutions, and/or organizations. Structuralist analysis is interested in the social, political, and economic networks that form between and among individuals (Landman, 2006). Structures manifest themselves in a variety of forms both at the domestic and at the international level. Politically and economically, structures include class and class coalitions, and institutions like business organizations, political parties and global ones like the United Nations, World Trade Organization and the General Agreement on Tariffs and Trade. Individual actors are not completely free agents capable of determining particular outcomes. Rather, individuals are embedded in relational structures that shape their identities, interests and interactions. But one must not forget that the setting up of SEZs is propelled by the historical dynamics of neoliberalism and the need for expanding markets.

The term "violence" can be defined, in general terms, as "needs-deprivation" (Galtung, 1969) or as "avoidable insults to basic human needs" (Galtung, 1969). Structural violence is the process of deprivation of needs. Simply put, it is violence embodied by a structure, or violence that operates regardless of intent (Galtung, 1969). It is characterized politically by repression, and economically by exploitation.

Galtung, at first, defines violence as "avoidable impairment of fundamental human needs or, to put it in more general terms, the impairment of human life, which lowers the actual degree to which someone is able to meet their needs below that which would otherwise be possible". He constructs a typology of violence, composed of three categories: personal, structural, and cultural. He asserts that structural violence, as opposed to personal or direct violence is indirect, in that there may not be any person who directly harms another person in the structure. The violence is built into the structure and shows up as unequal power and consequently as unequal life chances. The power to decide over the distribution of resources is unevenly distributed, which is the pivotal causal factor of structural inequalities. Because structural causes are responsible for constrained agency, it leads to behavioral violence. It is the effect of structures on individual agency that results in the gap between potential and actual fulfillment of rights.

Structural violence refers to a form of violence based on the systematic ways in which a given social structure or social institution "kills people," by preventing them from meeting their basic needs. Hunger and poverty are two prime examples of what is described as structural violence –physical and psychological harm that results from exploitive and unjust social, political and economic systems (Gilman, 1983). Life spans and quality of life are reduced when people are socially dominated, politically oppressed, or economically exploited. Structural violence, inevitably, produces conflict and often direct violence, including racial violence, terrorism, genocide, and war. It is the causing of harm by the inflexibility and rigidity of rules of the structure in dealing with difference.

The notion of structural violence was first articulated by Johan Galtung; it is conceptually and empirically separable from behavioral violence in six ways (Galtung, 1969). First, violence can be physical as well as psychological, affecting the body and the soul. Second, violence may be contained within rewards and not simply punishments. Third, violence exists even though someone is not hurt. Conflictive behavior, such as the issuing of credible threats to others' interests and values, the destruction of property and forced displacement can dissuade people from acting volitionally, obstruct a realization of potential and therefore do violence. Fourth, violence is present even when there is no subject-to-object relationship – no overt and distinguishable goal incompatibility, in other words. For instance, institutional racism within many large organizations limits the potential of individuals from minority backgrounds. Fifth, violence emerges from non-violent intentions. Sixth, violence is latent as well as manifest and includes many of the results of the international system's normal operation.

The theory of structural violence is a way to understand the "exploitation" and displacement caused by SEZs. Structural violence yields a complex picture of inequality as it considers economic, political, and social factors. Applying the theory of structural violence to the SEZ discourse illuminates the marginalized and neglected class of people whose very existence is at stake with the establishment of SEZs.

The Political Economy of SEZs in India

Zones or geographically delimited enclaves within a country are products of the process of globalization. The first of such modern zones was set up at Shannon in Ireland in 1956. These zones are distinguished from the rest of the land in terms of their specific administrative authority, benefits enjoyed by industries located in them and availability of better business facilities. Depending upon their specific purposes and economic and administrative regulations, a zone is called a Free Trade Zone (FTZ), an Export Processing Zone (EPZ), a Free Zone (FZ), an Industrial Estate (IE), a Free Port, an Urban Enterprise Zone, a Free Economic Zone (FEZ) or a Special Economic Zone (SEZ). India was one of the first countries in Asia to recognize the effectiveness of the Export Processing Zone (EPZ) model in promoting exports, with Asia's first EPZ set up in Kandla in 1965. With a view to overcome the shortcomings experienced on account of the multiplicity of controls and clearances, absence of world-class infrastructure, and an unstable fiscal regime and to attract larger foreign investments in India, the Special Economic Zone Policy was announced in April 2000.

A neoliberal revolution came in the year 2000 when SEZs were incorporated into the EXIM Policy of India. Five years later, the SEZ Act, 2005, was also introduced and in 2006 SEZ Rules were formulated. According to the Act, a Special Economic Zone is a specially demarcated area of land, owned and operated by a private company, which is deemed to be foreign territory for the purpose of trade, duties and tariffs. SEZs enjoy exemptions from customs duties, income tax, sales tax and service tax. They are projected as duty free areas for the purpose of trade, operations, duty and tariffs. SEZ units are self-contained and integrated, having their own infrastructure and support services.

SEZs have been implemented using a variety of institutional structures across the world, ranging from fully public institutions (government operated, government developed, government regulated) to "fully" private ones (private operated, private developed, public regulated). In many cases, public sector operators and developers act as quasi-government agencies, in that they have a pseudo-corporate institutional structure and budgetary autonomy. SEZs are often developed under a public-private partnership arrangement, in which the public sector provides some level of support (provision of off-site infrastructure, equity investment, soft loans, bond issues, etc) to enable a private sector developer to obtain a reasonable rate of return on the project.

SEZs can be sector specific or multi product enclaves. They help in the development of infrastructure of surrounding areas, provide employment to people, and make exports more viable. The government argues that this will help the country's products to become more competitive by providing all round development of regions. Within SEZs, a unit may be set-up for the manufacture of goods and for other activities including processing, assembling, trading, repairing, reconditioning, making of gold, silver and platinum jewellery etc. The area requirement for setting up a SEZ varies from 10 hectares to 1000 hectares, depending on the type of SEZ. There are more than 500 SEZs in India, at various stages of growth and maturity – functional, or notified, or formally approved and or ones which have been cleared in-principle.

The main features of an Indian SEZ are: a modern harbor, an airport, financial institutions, a vibrant industrial city with abundant supply of skilled and semi-skilled manpower, well connected with network of public transport, local railways and cabs, pollution free environment with proper drainage and sewage system, in-house customs clearance facilities and uninterrupted power supply. Goods and services coming into a SEZ from the domestic tariff area or DTA (area outside of the SEZ, where the laws of the country are applicable) are treated as exports from India and goods and services rendered from the SEZ to the DTA are treated as imports into India. There are simplified procedures for development, operation, and maintenance of the Special Economic Zones and for setting up units and conducting business. There is single window clearance for setting up of a SEZ.

The main *promise and rationale* of the SEZ Act, 2005 of India are described in the guidelines provided in Section 5: (a) *generation of additional economic activity;* (b) *promotion of exports of goods and services;* (c) *promotion of investment from domestic and foreign sources;* (d) *creation of employment opportunities;* (e) *development of infrastructure facilities; and (e) maintenance of sovereignty and integrity of India, the security of the State and friendly relations with foreign States.*

Violence of SEZs

Structural violence is inherent in a situation in which the intentioned or unintended result is injury and destruction. It becomes a form of institutionalized social injustice when development projects like SEZs bring about displacement and loss of livelihood of the weaker sections of the society. The notion of increased production and creation of growth has always been seen as being in the national interest, with intention to develop society. Resources are extracted by the elites of society and those who are "resource poor" have no involvement in this process, which takes away the little they had, and in the process reduces them to "objects" of development.

The doctrine of "eminent domain" is invoked by the state and for the "greater common good," private and community land is acquired from the people, to facilitate the SEZs, which invariably necessitate involuntary resettlement of people, or in other words, they necessitate displacement. Land-grabbing policies are tools of exploitation and are anti-people, thus involving violence. Even as a SEZ creates wealth for a few, it leaves the others with an irreparable sense of loss and impoverishment and violence wrought in their wake. And when these people make an attempt at resistance, they inevitably come into conflict with the law. Already marginalized, they are further faced with state power, reinforced by wealth out to create more of it, and lastly by an educated urban middle class impregnated with the rhetoric whereof development, synonymous with progress and modernization, is the panacea for all the ills of the third world.

There are many dimensions of this structural violence: oppression, humiliation and discrimination along the lines of class and ethnicity, and regular harassment, violence and torture by arms of the State. For the poor and marginalized population, the violence of poverty, hunger and abysmal living conditions has been worsened by the structural violence that they encounter daily. There is also an unprecedented attack on the access of the marginalized and poor to common property resources.

The neoliberal turn in the policy framework of the Indian state has further worsened the problems of economic vulnerability and social deprivation. Whatever little access the poor had to forests, land, rivers, common pastures, village tanks and other common property resources, to cushion their inevitable slide into poverty, has been captured by the Indian state in the guise of SEZs and other development projects related to mining, industrial development, Information Technology parks, etc. Berger's (1974) phrase "Pyramids of Sacrifice" refers to huge structures built upon the lives of victims. SEZs are also such structures which have rendered many homeless and pauperized. The cost of development is borne by the underdogs. The political ethics of development involves a "calculus of pain". SEZs involve prosperity of certain groups and sacrifices and violent suffering for the rest of the population. The former reap benefits and the latter bear the cost. For development to be just, this predicament has to be looked at afresh, from the standpoint of those who are victims and sufferers.

These economic enclaves get laborers – daily wage, temporary and permanent – from the neighboring villages and towns. This kind of contact and the relations of production lead to the formation of "ghettos" with a distinct "culture of poverty." The cultural values of the rich, be they foreign or domestic, become homogenous in their striving to make more money by producing more surplus value and reinvestment of the accumulated profit to get more profit. In this process, the rich inflict structural violence on the poor. This is an imperialism of a new kind, in which the cultural values of the more powerful class are gradually imposed on the weaker class, leading to "particularization" of dominant values and colonization of the culture of the poor by the rich. This leads to more deprivation, violence and therefore resistance.

Thus a conflictive situation is seen in such circumstances, in which damage that occurs to individuals or groups is due to differential access to social resources, and due to the normal operation of the social system (Webb, 1986). Denial of rights and needs such as economic well-being, dignity, equality, education and so on, emerges from everyday activities and from the actions of people who are rarely directly violent. The establishment of SEZs further increases disparities in income levels, intensifying class differentiation and marginalization of the poor. There is a growing disparity between those who are rich and getting richer and those who are poor and getting poorer.

The statutory requirements of seeking clearances from the Department of Environment or Forests are not followed. Furthermore, the actual stakeholders i.e. the "public" is never consulted before finalizing the projects and the often mentioned formula of people's participation has become a travesty of people's lives.

According to Galtung (1990) structural violence leads to exploitation of the "underdogs" by the "top dogs". In economic exchange and in the transformation of the world, some referred to as "top dogs", benefit a great deal more from interactions in the structure than the underdogs or losers, who suffer from growing displacement and marginalization from the global economy. The setting up of SEZs seems to institutionalize the economic elites' "penetration" (defined by Galtung as "implanting the top dog inside the underdog"), "segmentation" ("giving the underdog only a very partial view of what goes on"), "marginalization" ("keeping the underdogs on the outside"), and "fragmentation" (keeping the underdogs away from each other"). The infiltration of "outsiders" in the land of the natives, keeping the people at a distance from the decisions which affect their lives, relegating them and dividing them from within, are acts of violence that the developers of SEZs perpetrate. Together these processes increase the exploitation of the weak and create greater levels of disharmony and discontent in the country. This structural violence facilitates behavioral violence as a response to the inequalities and exploitation that underpin structural violence. Nandigram and Singur, were incidents which suggest that structural violence contains the capacity to provoke agential violence from the deprived and displaced groups.

Moreover, there is an on-going debate on the violation of

democratic principles in these SEZs. Are these SEZs becoming new corporate City-States? Many of the SEZs, like the Mahamumbai SEZ (to be built by Reliance Industries) will be like a mid-sized city, over 100 sq km in area (the size of Chandigarh). There will be no elected local government. A government appointed "Development Commissioner" will govern the SEZ with the main aim of facilitating economic growth. SEZs have been declared "Public Utilities" under the Industrial Disputes Act, making collective bargaining and strikes illegal. Infrastructure, like power, roads and water supply has been guaranteed to investors and developers, not to people of the region. Several lakh people may be living or working inside a SEZ. In some cases the developer may have the right to tax the population in order to provide essential services. The Constitutional tenability of private monopolies running local governments (for a sizeable cluster of the urban population) without being elected is questionable. All the non-economic laws of the land under the Indian Penal Code and the Criminal Procedure Code would be applicable to SEZs. However, internal security will be the responsibility of the developer. Would the SEZs turn ultimately into sovereign city-states – treasure islands of prosperity in a sea of poverty and misery – unaccountable to the vast majority of citizens in the neighborhood, is a pertinent question (Shrivastava, 2008).

How does displacement constitute structural violence? Displacement is a multidimensional phenomenon not confined to physical relocation; it reduces the quality of life of the communities to sub-human conditions. In this context displacement refers not only to those who are forced to physically relocate in order to make way for the project and its related aspects but also includes those who are displaced from their resource base and livelihoods. It is commonly experienced in the loss of land and the disruption of social and economic relationships (Bartolome *et al,* 2009). Thus it becomes a manifestation of violence.

Value Losses: Human and Environmental Cost

With the creation of SEZs, the core values of "well being" (material, life and health sustenance, esteem, freedom, equity, participation and empowerment, and identity and meaning) are denied to the people who are displaced in the process. The struggle against displacement has thus become the struggle against the larger politics of globalization. Displacement is not confined to physical removal of one from his house, it can be a deprivation from productive land, or other income generating assets, the displacement from collectivities causes an economic crisis for all or most of those affected with sudden disarticulation and sometimes also triggers a political crisis (Cernea, 1999). It is a complex phenomenon, not a one-time event but a series of happenings affecting human lives in myriad ways (Baxi, 1989). For the displaced people, there is loss of livelihood and traditional lands, demolition of homes, loss of social networks, severance from an eco-system that sustained them earlier and, above all, a feeling of powerlessness and insecurity concerning the future. Their ethos and lifestyle is dismantled and denigrated because of creation of SEZs because of their strong attachments with the land. Many a times, there are multiple displacements of people – successive displacement of the same families from one place to another, following execution of development projects in each area.

Displacement and relocation, which are traumatic from both the economic and the cultural points of view, result in a host of socio-economic effects. From a predominantly non-monetized economy to a money-dominated one, and from a relatively isolated cultural existence to one in which other cultures start imposing themselves, the transition is painful (Lasgorceix and Kothari, 2009). For cultivation at the new rehabilitation site, quality and fertility of the new land is important. For communities dependent on livestock, availability of grazing lands and fodder is crucial. For communities heavily dependent on non-timber forest produce or aquatic produce in their traditional locations, there is often a severe loss since the resettlement sites do not have the same kind or level of resources. Availability of water sources at the new site is another important aspect which affects agriculture and horticulture. Living in another cultural environment with other values and points of reference can be traumatic and disturbing.

Local economies are dismantled with the creation and expansion of industrial capitalism. The attack on the local takes the form of primitive accumulation and the gains to the capitalist that of rent appropriation. Primitive accumulation involves dispossession of the commons – land, water, forest, knowledge, technology, etc. – that are shared at the community level (Patnaik, 2008; Basu, 2008). Thus the process of establishing SEZs in India is essentially a classic unfolding of the process of "accumulation by dispossession," where the violence of capitalism is subsumed in the rhetoric of development (Banerjee-Guha, 2008). A major part of the growth envisaged in the SEZs is through real estate and infrastructure development. These kinds of corporatized development helps consumer culture grow, creating more and more deprivation and unrest among the marginalized.

The growth of employment in the organized sector since the inception of economic reforms in 1991 has been negligible as far as the poor and the unskilled laborers are concerned. With more automation, organized services require limited supplies of labor. SEZs attract modern industry and services in order to succeed. To that extent they are unlikely to generate too many jobs. Moreover, the few jobs that will be generated will be for highly skilled labor, usually not available in the countryside. Furthermore, if the experience of existing SEZs in places like NOIDA is to be evaluated, the working conditions – poor wages, non-existent benefits, long working hours, occupational hazards, discrimination and so on – under which people are employed inevitably violate human rights, apart from keeping the benefits of growth away from the poor. A study of the Nokia SEZ (Dutta, 2009) reveals the enormous costs that the state government has incurred to attract Nokia to invest in the state and the few benefits such investments have created.

Development of SEZs has meant displacement and pauperization of the tribals. Apart from the loss of land, living and lifestyle of generations, displacement causes other traumatic, psychological and socio-cultural consequences, making their life even more miserable and impoverished (Mohanty, 2005). In the name of development, tribals are displaced from their traditional habitats and livelihoods with little or no rehabilitation, and are rendered destitute, bewildered and pauperized by the development process. They are pushed into a vortex of increasing assetlessness, unemployment, debt bondage and hunger, due to loss of access to traditional sources of livelihood *viz.*, land, forests, rivers, pastures, cattle etc.

Also, any loss of access to traditional sources of livelihood marginalizes women in the labor market. It is only when land and other sources are replaced that women, at least partially, regain their economic status. Women not only suffered in terms of health and nutrition, they also lose the capacity to provide a secure future for their children. By resorting to seasonal migration they have unwittingly denied their children access to school, health care, child welfare, and other welfare services (Hemadri, 1999). Furthermore, considering widow, deserted and unmarried adult daughters as dependents, ends their right to claim separate or independent rehabilitation packages, with no land allotment in their names.

Ironically, the displaced lot, apparently, do not include the landless, the non-asset class, the seasonal farmers, the fishermen, the boatmen, small shopkeepers, and those engaged in the creation of works of art, culture and handicraft, in the affected village. They are excluded from the benefits of rehabilitation packages. Besides the profound vulnerability of the landless agricultural workers, there are people like the destitute, beggars, the uncared for, aged, women victims of violence and abandonment, the disabled, leprosy patients, the mentally ill, and children deprived of adult care, who are in any case condemned to the margins of society, and are likely to be the first to fall by the wayside (Hemadri, 1999).

Displacement forces people to leave their usual habitation, to which they are used to; in doing so they leave behind, besides their personal belongings, the common utility assets, the social bonds and security, an essential part of their life. Not only are land-owners evacuated but the landless agricultural laborers, carpenters, blacksmiths, cobblers, barbers, tailors and so on, who too depend on these land and the village society lose their livelihood as well. Common properties like grazing land, ponds, wells, sacred grooves, worship places, playgrounds, and fuel sources are lost for the village; on the other hand, in urban context, people lose their places of work; this especially true for the self-employed, like hawkers and vendors. The worst form of social impoverishment is caused due to loss of networks which are built up over generations; people who are used to traditional ways of living are exposed to entirely new and alien living conditions and environments that are hostile to them.

People confront each other and fights start within families for the compensation money; the callous settlement of different ethnic and caste groups leads to growth of inter-community hostility. Many are rendered jobless and even if jobs are offered, they find it beneath their dignity, once landowners, now having to work as laborers. The affected people have no political voice as they are resettled in new, fragmented conditions where there is lack of uniformity; thus the living conditions at different places of resettlement are different. Common interests have vanished, leaving the marginalized ones further on the periphery.

Special Economic Zones have, besides displacement, produced another vulnerable group, the urban poor or the new proletariat. The rural populations, which are displaced or those who move out in search of livelihood (forced migration) end up living at the periphery of urban society. A land owner in the village becomes an urban laborer, thus creating a new class of people in the urban social hierarchy *viz.* the slum dwellers. The person who had already lost his usual life and livelihood, thereby, also loses his life on the margins.

Another allegation on the SEZs has been that they are accentuating regional and sectoral disparity and imbalances. Most of the approved SEZs are in high-income states. States like Bihar, Assam, Arunachal Pradesh and Manipur do not have SEZs. SEZs connected with Information Technology have proliferated post-2005 and provide the bulk of employment. These SEZs are generally close to already existing urban centers. SEZs have not helped spread industrial or service activities to remote areas or to rural hinterlands. Moreover, the benefits of such investments are also challenged.

There are controversies regarding snatching of arable or cultivated land, and about the buying of land at very discounted rates, from farmers or poor people, and then selling it to corporates at exorbitant prices. The total amount of land to be acquired across India is 150,000 hectares. This land – predominantly agricultural and typically multicropped – is capable of producing close to 1 million tons of foodgrains. If SEZs are seen to be successful in the future and more cultivated land is acquired, they might endanger food security in India.

The environmental costs of setting up SEZs would be no less. SEZs would lead to the destruction huge chunks of forest cover causing irreversible loss to varieties of flora and fauna, besides the land area. The pollution (air, water, soil and noise) caused by the industries accentuates the miseries of the present generation as well as the generations to come. Added to this pollution by industries and urban centers, is the garbage and toxic waste that is generated over time. At the new rehabilitation site, the main environmental impact is the destruction or degradation of natural ecosystems. This is due to clearance for cultivation and houses, roads etc.

Despite being on the seismic map of the world and even after facing numerous fatal tremors, SEZs are not planned and constructed in accordance with safety norms with respect to earthquakes. Many of the SEZs are planned in coastal regions which face cyclones every now and then. No preventive measure is seen at any level of governance, be it policy choice, planning, implementation or enforcement. The philosophy seems to be – redressal after disaster has occurred. Much of the loss of life and property is caused not because of the intensity of the disaster but due to absence of efficient post disaster rescue, resettlement and rehabilitation (immediate, short-run and long-run) operations.

Compensation for Lost Values?

The government promises "humane" displacement followed by relief and rehabilitation. But till date there is virtually no uniform law for rehabilitation and resettlement in India. 'Resettlement' refers to the process of physical relocation of displaced people, while 'rehabilitation' connotes the restoration of lost economic and social abilities. All that exists today in terms of law and policy is the Land Acquisition Act, 1894 that lays down that the government is not bound to provide a displaced person anything but cash compensation. The Rehabilitation and Resettlement (R&R) Policy of 2007 clearly mentions the principle of three "minima." These are: (i) minimize displacement; (ii) minimize acquisition of land, and (iii) minimize usage of agricultural land for non-agricultural use. Under the new policy, a set of terms and conditions have been given therefore projects which involve physical displacement of 400 or more families *en masse* in the plains or of 200 or more families in tribal or hilly areas. This policy has several components. It introduces the concept of Social Impact Assessment (SIA) along with the already present norm of Environmental Impact Assessment. The SIA would involve public hearings on displacement-related issues, loss of livelihood, compensation, effects on family and so on. For projects in tribal areas, a mandatory Tribal Development Plan involving a program for development of alternate fuel, fodder and non-timber forest produce on non-forest land within five years after displacement is called for. Furthermore, for agricultural workers, at least one person in each family shall be given employment or a one-time "rehabilitation grant" equivalent to 750 days minimum agricultural wages. If it's a corporate project, a fifth of the compensation will be in the form of the company's shares. But the question remains that when rehabilitation of people displaced by dams like Hirakud, built way back in 1950s is not yet complete, what will happen to those displaced by SEZs? Moreover, there is always a discrepancy between policy and practice, between formulation and implementation of policies.

SEZs have accentuated the negative aspects of displacement, such as lack of information, failure to prepare in advance a comprehensive plan for rehabilitation, the undervaluation of compensation and its payment in cash, failure to restore lost assets or livelihoods, traumatic and delayed relocation, problems at relocation sites, multiple displacement, and neglect of the special vulnerabilities of the most disadvantaged groups etc (Mander, 2003). The problem of setting a fair market value for land is also a concern.

Michael Cernea (1999) had identified many interlinked potential risks intrinsic to displacement: landlessness, joblessness, homelessness, marginalization, food insecurity, increased morbidity and mortality, loss of access to common property and services, social disarticulation, differential risks, and the risk to host populations. As a result of the convergent and cumulative effect of development-induced displacement, entailing rapid onset of impoverishment, is not limited to the community of the displaced but are risks incurred by the local (regional) economy as well, to which they may inflict major loss and disruption. The general policy of compensation does not fit into the welfare schemes of a government founded on the principles of socialism, and serves only to mitigate immediate desolation while ignoring long run and permanent solutions to problems.

The only way to save good agricultural land is to let developers concentrate on acquiring dry non-paddy fields and single cropped areas. The landholders and non-landholders have to be compensated properly in monetary terms, and in addition each family has to be provided with employment, in exchange for the land and livelihood from which they are being alienated.

Resistance and Violent Conduct

Thus, the introduction of SEZs in India has resulted in dispossession from agricultural land and has affected the livelihood of farmers at large. The political landscape of India presents small and large people's movements that fight back the appropriation of their natural resources, livelihood and means of survival by their own governments, and large national and international corporations. The villagers in India, whether they are from Nandigram in West Bengal, Raigad in Maharashtra or Santhankulam in Tamil Nadu express their strong discontentment with the establishment of SEZs. But the resistance against SEZ in India became massive when political parties and social activists also joined the farmers. The dissent, uproar, and opposition from the farmers have led to behavioral violence of the farmers against the state.

These resistance movements have been across regions in India. In the southern region, Muthanga forest land struggle, Waynad, Kerala *by* Adivasi Gothra Maha Sabha and farmers' rally against Reliance SEZ in Navi Mumbai. In western and central India, farmers protested against SEZ in Raigad, against land acquisition by Reliance in Greater Mumbai. In the eastern region, there is a struggle in Singur and Nandigram (West Bengal), against SEZs and displacement; adivasis are struggling in Jadugoda against uranium mining and displacement. In the north-east region, there have been people's movements in Doyang and Tongani, Assam against forcible eviction from forests. In the northern region, farmers protested against the Reliance SEZ in Jhajjar, Haryana and farmers are also struggling against land acquisition for Trident SEZ in Barnala, Punjab.

There have been varying responses to the implementation of SEZs across states in India. The policy implementation gets shaped by the regional political economy. A recent study of the SEZs in Tamil Nadu (Vijayabaskar, 2010) reveals that despite being home to a large number of SEZs, Tamil Nadu has been one state which has not witnessed confrontational or systematic resistance to SEZs in general, and land acquisition in particular, on a scale comparable to states with a similar history of SEZs. There are clear structural reasons for the willingness of farmers to give up their land and move away from agriculture. But states like Tamil Nadu have been exceptional cases, where eviction from land has not been resisted. Massive resistance to land acquisition in Goa compelled the state government to ask for denotification of the SEZs that were supposed to be set up. The protests by farmers in Singur led to the shifting of Tata's small car plant to Gujarat. Other responses to SEZs, including cases of agential violence are discussed below.

The violence in Nandigram is a well known incident related to SEZs. Nandigram is a rural area in Purba Medinipur district of West Bengal. In 2007 the West Bengal government decided to allow the Indonesia-based Salim Group to set up a "chemical hub" at Nandigram under the SEZ policy. Farmers of that village were against it. So, by orders of the Left Front government, on 14 March, 2007, more than 3,000 heavily armed policemen stormed into Nandigram. The main objective was to remove the protestors in order to expropriate 10,000 acres of land for the SEZ. The police shot dead at least 14 villagers and wounded 244 persons including children and women (Bandyopadhyay, 2007).

The farmers of Jamnagar have moved court. In November

2006, farmers from Jamnagar district in Gujarat went to the High Court of Gujarat and later to the Supreme Court, in order to challenge the setting-up of a 10,000-acre (approx. 4,000-ha) SEZ by Reliance Infrastructure. They claimed that the acquisition of large tracts of agricultural land in the villages of the district not only violated the Land Acquisition Act of 1894, but was also in breach of public interest. This led the Government to "consider" putting a ceiling on the maximum land area that can be acquired for multi-product zones and it was decided to "go slow' in approving SEZs.

The Mundra SEZ is another enclave situated on the northern shore of the Gulf of Kutch with the Adani Group as its developer. This SEZ will cause displacement and will destroy the livelihoods of fishermen. There are other serious concerns, such as the destruction of mangroves, affecting the marine ecology of the Gulf of Kutch, according to environmentalists. Fishermen in the settlements along the coastline practice two forms of fishing, *lagadia* and *pagadia*. Their settlements, which lack even basic infrastructure, are not recognized by authorities. According to the Gujarat fisheries department census (1997-98), these fishing settlements have a population of 3,979, from 705 households.[1] Because neither the government nor the Adani Group recognizes the presence of these settlements, the people fear they will be evicted. Not all fisherfolk, however, live along the coastline. There are around 10 villages along the perimeter of the SEZ from where fisherfolk commute daily, by foot or by cycle, to practice *pagadia*. Those in the Shekhadiya village are outraged because an airstrip has been constructed across their route to the sea. The government argues that the SEZ will bring about a positive transformation for the local communities. It says that agricultural land in the state is limited because of scanty rainfall. Moreover many hectares of mangroves have been cleared for the SEZ. This may have significant environmental and economic implications. Deep within the gulf, the waters around the Mundra port gets recycled slowly. Any pollution-causing leak from the industry would take a long time to be flushed out, stagnating, suffocating and killing marine life.

People fear that the industries will deplete local aquifers that sustain the double-cropped agricultural system. Gujarat fishermen have challenged the allocation of 600 acre of land for the multi-product SEZ as it comes under the protected maritime zone.

The above examples show the controversies associated with the SEZs. The anti-people land-grabbing, and the plundering of natural resources leads to violent development. Moreover, there are cases filed against activists of anti-SEZ movements although people of a free modern polity can protest. But there are positive outcomes from such violent actions and reactions of the threatened. The violent conduct brings about a reduction in structural violence and thus the sum-total of violence is reduced.

Conclusion

Special Economic Zones are duty-free economic enclaves with streamlined procedures, tax breaks and good infrastructure to lure investors in export industries. They are seen as vehicles for inducing export oriented growth in backward regions within a state. The main objectives of SEZs are attracting Foreign Direct Investments (FDI), increasing exports, enabling transfer of modern technology, creating incentives for infrastructure and accelerating economic growth.

The SEZs are promoting the expropriation of community resources for the profit of domestic and multinational corporations. Violence occurs when a number of SEZ projects which have no "public purpose" attached, usurp land from property owners, with the help of the Land Acquisition Act, at below the market value of these properties. Even in the case of SEZs that are genuinely for public purposes, there is a considerable difference between the market value of the property and the value that the land acquisition officer pays to the land owners. It is also argued that the relocation and rehabilitation of land owners displaced by the under the Act, is not followed up adequately.

Development means a realization of human potential and the criteria to judge it is whether life is happier, more fruitful and enjoyable for an individual. The SEZ policy is inherently biased and prejudiced; its emphasis is on industrialization, science and technology, ruthless exploitation of natural resources and letting loose of market forces, completely ignoring and eroding the cultural and social sensibilities, identities and distinctiveness of subjects. Thus, the establishment of SEZs is another way of alienating the poor from the developmental process. Moreover, the role of democracy as a political system has been neglected. The raging impact of SEZs and the despair and despondency caused by displacement, or the failure to address the issues of resettlement, rehabilitation and reparation of the displaced, are examples of structural violence. Instead of people-centered development, in which people are empowered to make their own choices and relevance of local knowledge and values is emphasized, development through creation of SEZs is definitely anti-poor and anti-nature. This structural violence leads to an overt and relational kind of violence with the affected people taking the law into their hands.

Furthermore, there are many apprehensions against the establishments of SEZs. Given the concessions on import duties, there are likely to be foreign exchange losses (rather than gains). This results in loss of public revenue and creation of serious economic imbalances. There may be little generation of new activity, and thus employment. Large-scale land acquisition would lead to not only displacement of farmers and others, but would also have serious implications for food security. There could be misuse of acquired land by the developers, for real estate. The establishment of SEZs involves many violations of the law[2] : it violates the letter and spirit of the Indian Constitution; it infringes the fundamental rights of the citizen guaranteed in Part III of the Constitution; labor laws are either relaxed or not applied;

environmental clearance is not needed; the Panchayat Raj Act, 1996 for local self government, is violated; laws granting rights and control to adivasi communities over their land are violated. Many international conventions concerning human rights are also violated. In the SEZs, the sacred law and the Constitution of the country are overlooked (Ali, 2007). Doing away with the regulatory hurdles leads to the making of SEZs as exploitation zones. Instead of being for public good, SEZs are producing goods for few at the cost of the rest of the population.

When people protest, the response of the State is to crack down on peaceful protestors, levy false charges against the leaders, to arrest them and often to resort to police firing and violence, so as to terrorize them. We only need to remember Singur, Nandigram, Kalinganagar and countless other instances where peaceful and democratic forms of protest were crushed by the state with ruthless force. It is, thus, the action of the State that blocks off all forms of democratic protest and forces the poor and dispossessed to take up arms to defend their rights. Instead of addressing the source of the conflict and the genuine grievances of the marginalized people, the Indian state opts for the extremely myopic option of launching a military offensive.

The contemporary development process has its beneficiaries as well victims. But the victims, sufferers and the threatened outnumber the beneficiaries. Economic growth does not necessarily ensure equitable distribution of "well-being." This is the predicament of development. Development is inevitable, but it has to be unbiased and equal in its manifestations and humane in its consequences. The socio-cultural costs of developmental projects like SEZs can be minimized, if not eliminated. The neoliberal policies of the state marginalize the poor and the underprivileged. When a centre of prosperity develops in the vicinity of poverty, the widening disparity creates more and more tension, cultural conflict and violence. This definitely increases pain and frustration among the displaced lot, a manifestation of all the problems of core-periphery relationships and unequal exchange. There is enough empirical evidence and theoretical grounds to suggest that the SEZ policy can lead to widening of disparities between classes and regions, social conflict and breakdown of democratic institutions, leading to structural violence. The socio-cultural costs, the feasibility and desirability of SEZs, have to be studied thoroughly, debated and looked at afresh.

Endnotes

1. India Environmental Portal available at *www.indiaenvironmentalportal.org.in/node/31432* accessed on 21.04.10.
2. Adapted from "SEZs and Land Acquisition: Factsheet for an Unconstitutional Economic Policy" prepared by Citizens' Research Collective, New Delhi, March 2007, available at *http://www.sacw.net/Nation/sezland_eng.pdf* accessed on April 23, 2010.

References

Ali, R. (2007). Economic Zones of India and the "China Model": What is going to happen? [*http://sanhati.com/articles/231* (Accessed on April 23, 2010)].

Arunachalam, P. (2008). *Special Economic Zones in India: Principles, Problems and Prospects.* New Delhi: Serials Publications.

Bandyopadhyay, D. (2007). Buddha's Killing Fields of Nandigram. *Mainstream,* Vol. XLV, No. 50.

Banerjee-Guha, Swapna. (2008, November 22). Space Relations of Capital and Significance of New Economic Enclaves: SEZs in India. *Economic and Political Weekly.*

Basu, P.K. (2008). *Globalization: An Anti-Text: A Local View.* New Delhi: Aakar Books.

Baxi, U. (1989). Notes on Constitutional and Legal Aspects of Displacement and Rehabilitation. In M. Walter Fernandez and E. Ganguly Thakral (Eds.), *Development, Displacement and Rehabilitation.* New Delhi: Indian Social Institute.

Berger, P. (1974). *Pyramids of Sacrifice.* London: Penguin.

Bartolome, L.J. *et.al.* (2009). Displacement, Resettlement, Rehabilitation, Reparation, and Development. *Journal of Environmental Management,* Vol. 90, Supplement 3, S203-S207.

Bufacchi, V. (2005). Two Concepts of Violence. *Political Studies Review*, Vol. 3, Issue 2, 193-204.

Cernea, M.M. (1999). Development's Painful Social Costs: Introductory Study. In S. Parasuraman (Ed.), *The Development Dilemma: Displacement in India.* London: Macmillan Press.

Cernea, M.M. (1999). Why Economic Analysis is Essential to Resettlement: A Sociologist's View. In Michael Cernea (Ed.) *The Economics of Involuntary Resettlement: Questions and Challenges.* Washington DC: World Bank.

Cernea, M.M. (2000, October 7). Risks, Safeguards and Reconstruction: A Model for Population Displacement and Resettlement, *Economic and Political Weekly.*

Cernea, M.M. (2006). Re-examining "Displacement": A Redefinition of Concepts in Development and Conservation Policies, *Social Change*, Vol. 36 (1), 8-35.

Chatterjee, A. and Jetli, K.N. (2009). *Industry and Infrastructure Development in India since 1947.* New Delhi: New Century Publications.

Dutta, M. (2009, October 3, 9). Nokia SEZ: The Public Price of Success. In *Economic and Political Weekly*, 23-25.

Engels, F. (1987). *Anti-Duhring*, in Karl Marx and Fredrich Engels, *Collected Works*, Vol. 25. New York: International Publishers.

Fanon, F. (1966). *The Wretched of the Earth.* New York: Grove.

Farmer, P. (2005). *Pathologies of Power.* Berkeley: University of California Press.

Galtung, J. (1969). Violence, Peace, and Peace Research, *Journal of Peace Research*, Vol. 6, No. 3. 167-191.

Galtung., J. (1990). Cultural Violence. *Journal of Peace Research.* Vol. 27, No. 3. 291-305.

Gasper, D. (2005). *The Ethics of Development.* New Delhi: Vistaar Publications.

Gilman, R. (1983). Structural Violence: Can we find genuine peace in a world with inequitable distribution of wealth among nations? *In Context.* Autumn 1983.

Government of India, (2009). [*http://sezindia.nic.in/html.*]

Hegel, G.W.F. (1977). *Phenomenology of Spirit.* Oxford: Oxford University Press.

Hemadri, R. *et. al.* (1999). Dams, Displacement, Policy and Law in

India, WCD Contributing paper for Thematic Review:1.3. [*http://planningcommission.nic.in/reports/articles/ncsxna/art_dam.pdf* (Accessed on April 25, 2010)].

Ho, K. (2007). Structural Violence as a Human Rights Violation, *Essex Human Rights Review*. Vol. 4, No. 2.

Infochange, (2010). [*www.infochangeindia.org/200703246254 / Other/ Features/FAQs- about- SEZs.html* (Accessed on April 23.2010)].

Jacoby, T. (2008). *Understanding Conflict and Violence: Theoretical and Interdisciplinary Approaches*. London: Routledge.

Kumar, R. (1989). *India's Export Processing Zones*, Delhi: Oxford University Press..

Landman, T. (2006). *Studying Human Rights.* New York: Routledge.

Mander, Harsh (2003). "A People Savaged and Drowned", *Frontline,* Vol. 20, Issue 08, April 12-25, 2003.

Marx, Karl (1976). *Capital: A Critique of Political Economy.*Vol. I. London: Penguin.

Mohanty, B. (2005, March 26). Displacement and Rehabilitation of Tribals. *Economic and Political Weekly*, 1318-1320.

Palit, A. and Bhattacharjee, S. (2008). *Special Economic Zones in India: Myth and Realities*. New Delhi: Anthem Press.

Patnaik, Utsa (2008). Imperialism, Resources and Food Security with reference to the Indian Experience. *Human Geography.* Vol. 1(1), 40-53.

Sampat, P. (2008). Special Economic Zones in India, *Economic and Political Weekly,* Vol. 43 (28), 25-30.

Seabrook, J. (1993). *Victims of Development, Resistance and Alternatives*. London: Verso.

Shrivastava, Aseem (2008). Towards Corporate City-States?. *Seminar,* No. 582.

Uvin, P. (1999). Development Aid and Structural Violence: The Case of Rwanda. *Development*, 42(3), 49-56.

Vijayabaskar, M. (2010). Saving Agricultural Labor from Agriculture: SEZs and Politics of Silence in Tamil Nadu, *Economic and Political Weekly*, Vol. XLV No. 6, February 6-12, 2010.

Webb, K. (1986). Structural Violence and the Definition of Conflict. In L. Pauling (Ed.), *World Encyclopaedia of Peace* 2. Oxford: Pergamon Press.

5

The Artifice of Modernity in Nation-Building: Analyzing the Case of "Postcolonial" Northeast India[1]

Neikolie Kuotsu

This paper uses the film *Yeh Gulistan Hamara*[2] as an entry point into the discourse of nation-building. Hence, remarks about the film will be made in some sections of the paper. However, engagement with the film text has been minimized to broaden the scope of the treatise. The paper delves into the idioms of nation-building adopted by the postcolonial elite and interrogates the efficacy of the project of modernity, and its implementation. The discourse is based on the premise that in post-independence India, the new political elite puts on the garb of the British colonizer. The idiom of nation building primarily takes two forms – that of a benevolent master with a civilizing mission to save the wretched natives, and that of a repressive state apparatus (Althusser, 1971). India's Northeast shares a peripheral relationship with the nation, which is manifested in its history and geopolitics. The region was subsumed under British India and continues to serve as a buffer zone between uncongenial neighboring nations. The problematic of constructing a pan-national identity is compounded by geographical location and heterogeneity of language, race, religion and socio-cultural practices. Thus, the political elite harp on about development and progress, basing themselves on the western notion of teleological progress from a feudal society to a modern nation-state. It is under this paradigm of nation-building that developmental projects have been implemented in Northeast India for the longest time. However, the persistence of dissident voices of the disaffected communities and the various insurgent identity struggles invites the ire of the State in the form of repressive military regimes. The outcome of this is a spiral of violence.

Yeh Gulistan Hamara

The film *Yeh Gulistan Hamara* tells the story of Vijay (Dev Anand), an engineer deputed by the Ministry of Home Affairs of independent India to the Northeastern frontier to build a bridge across the river Tushima. The region (known as Dihing in the film) is described as one of extreme backwardness. The bridge is to link the tribals to mainland India and bring about development. The good engineer arrives in Dihing and embarks on his "civilizing" mission as he begins construction of the bridge. He collaborates with Captain Barua to win over the feudal ruler and the tribals and convinces them that they would remain backward if they continue to be isolated from the rest of the country. The local feudal ruler obstinately thwarts the construction of the bridge and deploys the militants of the resistance movement led by Reni (Sharmila Tagore) to sabotage the construction work. Reni and her companions are caught by the security forces and yet go unpunished. The feudal ruler comes to believe that Vijay means well. Vijay gains popularity among the local children by teaching them to sing the nationalist song *Saare Jahan Se Achcha* and instills in them a sense of citizenship. He further gains the confidence of the feudal ruler by helping him procure arms from a foreign agent. However, when Vijay prevents the bridge from being destroyed by explosives, his loyalty to the feudal ruler is questioned and he is condemned to die. After a prolonged skirmish between the feudal ruler's supporters and Vijay's newfound supporters, the ruler and his men are defeated and overthrown. The bridge is built, and all is well in the once godforsaken land.

The State of Statism

> England, it is true, in causing a social revolution in Hindustan was actuated only by the vilest interests, and was stupid in her manner of enforcing them. But that is not the question. The question is, can mankind fulfill its destiny without a fundamental revolution in the social state of Asia? If not, whatever may have been the crimes of England she was the unconscious tool of history in bringing about that revolution. (Marx & Engels, 1959, p. 20)

The project of nation-building in postcolonial India uses the idioms of colonialism and derives its strategies from the western model of nationalism particularly the erstwhile British Raj (Chatterjee, 1999). The post-colonial elite took over from the British colonizer to gain control over the erstwhile semi-administered hill areas and princely states in northeast India. The task of integration was and continues to be a challenging one. For administrative convenience, various states were sporadically carved out to form a lose conglomeration of what is called the Northeast today. This continues to be a bone of contention between the various communities in the Northeast and New Delhi. The isolation of the Northeastern states began as a result of British imperialism, when the region was cut-off from its traditional trading partners – Bhutan, Myanmar and Indo-China (Baruah, 2004). The heterogeneous population only compounded the problem and called for a catch-all strategy of creating a pan-national consciousness based on common goals and interests. Ashis Nandy (2002, p. 3) posits that the modern nation-state is "suspicious of all cultural differences, not on the grounds of racial or ethnic prejudice, but on the grounds that such differences intervened between the 'liberated' individual and the republican state and interfered with the more professional aspect of statecraft". Under this predicament the stratagem to bridge differences and allay the fears of the diverse populace is by deploying the language of modernization. Endorsers of the project of modernity perceive it to be a harbinger of progress, reason, liberty, equality and fraternity as it were. The State promotes integration, which is based not so much on shared traditions or history but on the western notion of teleological progress mentioned earlier. This is achieved in ways that are, more often than not, antagonistic to the populace.

In the film *Yeh Gulistan Hamara*, Vijay the engineer represents the figure of the postcolonial Indian elite on a mission to build a bridge across the river Tushima so as to "civilize" the hapless tribals in the erstwhile North Eastern Frontier Agency. The construction of the bridge echoes Jawarharlal Nehru's project of democratic socialism marked by aggressive central planning and state investments, which emphasized upon building infrastructure and human capacity in a bid to uplift the nation. Such sentiments are outlined in his famous speech, "A Tryst with Destiny." Here is an excerpt:

> The future beckons to us. Whither do we go and what shall be our endeavor? To bring freedom and opportunity to the common man, to the peasants and workers of India; to fight and end poverty and ignorance and disease; to build up a prosperous, democratic and progressive nation, and to create social, economic and political institutions which will ensure justice and fullness of life to every man and woman.

According to Ashis Nandy (2002), two major elements in the ideology of the modern state are national security and development. The people inhabiting the nation are hegemonized into believing that the State acts in their best interest. They are but subjects, euphemistically referred to as citizens, in the project of nation-building. Herein comes the role of what Althusser called the ideological and the repressive state apparatuses. The ramifications of the state apparatuses will be dealt with as the paper progresses. At this point, I borrow from Frantz Fanon (1961) who argues that to project a national culture in the quest for nationalism is futile because the colonizer disparages it and labels the native's culture inferior and barbaric. He further mentions that the colonizer does not distinguish between the various nationalities such as the Angolan and the Nigerian, but clubs them under the umbrella term "nigger" or "savage". A parallel can be found in the language of the Indian postcolonial elite who, more often than not, labels the diverse communities of the Northeast as tribals and the region as "disturbed area" and "underdeveloped" in an overarching manner to legitimize the "developmental" mission and militarization.

As the opening sequence of the film *Yeh Gulistan Hamara* suggests, the postcolonial elite patronizingly takes up the mantle of a "civilizing agent whose magnanimity would rescue the Northeastern frontier from perpetual antiquity. The film, with its projection of the State's benevolence, can be seen as an archetype of the utopia of nationhood created by the ideological state apparatuses. The national media reinforces the state's ideology by setting agendas for public consumption in the process of which issues concerning the Northeast are constantly omitted. Thus, the landlocked Northeast region remains not just at the geographical periphery but also at the emotional periphery of the metropole. If the region finds its way into the national media, it is more often than not portrayed as an aberration. The othering of the Northeast is the rule rather than an exception. The gratuitous sensationalized coverage of the anguished women who disrobed themselves to protest against army excesses in Manipur is a case in point; it detracts from addressing the core issue. Modernization in India often becomes a hand-me-down version of western modernity, including its statecraft and technology, which serves to divide rather than to include. The downside of aspiring towards the Western model is that the binaries of self and other are perpetually at play. The stagist notion of progress makes the colonized believe that the past of the colonizer should be their present and the present of the colonizer would be their future. The contemporary geo-political problems in the Northeast ranging from struggles for identities, greater autonomy and sovereignty may be attributed to this aspiration that believes in an evolutionist paradigm. The longing to be in a position that is eternally elusive gives rise to romantic idealisms that translates into extreme violence perpetrated by insurgent militias and the state military. Modernization, the pet project of the Indian elite, is effectively implemented to appease as well as contain the dissenters. The very infrastructures of development such as roads and communication become sites to unleash a reign of state terror on civilians.

Western modernity does not make for a neat fit in a developing country like India that is witnessing varying degrees and scales of development. Thus, a regime of administration based on the logic of "us and them" is effectively established, which Partha Chatterjee (1999, pp. 16-18) has called "the rule of colonial difference". It may be argued that modernization often causes a split in colonialism between protective preservation of indigeneity and uplifting transformation. This predicament is manifested in the "language" used by the State in the practice of governmentality. Thus, protective policies like the "Inner Line" and the "Sixth Schedule", while protecting the indigenous people from being overwhelmed by outside influence, also turn out to be "protectively discriminating" by isolating the region from the rest of the country. In the process, minorities within minorities such as the smaller-tribes, non-tribals, women and non-indigenous have been disadvantaged. While the pre-colonial period was marked by a more fluid state of affairs unhindered by geographical demarcations, the colonial and post-colonial period had and continues to witness assertions of identity with linguistic, racial, religious and ethnic overtones that are becoming increasingly congealed. Today many of the Northeast states have organized insurgent movements that perceive the

Indian State as a colonizer and are extremely hostile to it. Insurgency took roots in Nagaland and Manipur in the early fifties, immediately after the establishment of the Republic of India, in Mizoram in the sixties, in Tripura in the seventies, while in the case of Assam it has arrived in the eighties. Meghalaya and Arunachal Pradesh are menacingly militant indeed but not yet insurgent (Bora, 1992). The manner in which the State deals with the various struggles for identity and insurgencies of the Northeast is indeed mimetic of the British Colonizer. This is well articulated by Homi K. Bhabha (1994, p. 86) who writes, "Colonial mimicry is the desire for a reformed, recognizable Other, as *a subject of a difference that is almost the same, but not quite*" (original emphasis). The patronizing approach of the State in constructing a modern and liberated subject citizen takes recourse in legislative sanctions that are legacies of colonialism.

Violence of Governing and the Governed

Frantz Fanon (1952, p. 60) in *Black Skin, White Masks* describes the pathological condition wrought by colonialism as, "The Negro enslaved by his inferiority, the white man enslaved by his superiority alike behave in accordance with a neurotic orientation." Fanon's notion of the neurosis of the colonizer and the colonized may be used to explain the carrot-and-stick policy of the State in Northeast India. Fanon describes the colonized's neurosis as obsessional and the colonizer's as phobic. However, I would extend this and turn it the other way round to explain the violent repercussions of the insurgent movements in the Northeast. Whereas on one hand, the Central Government obsessively doles out developmental packages to the Northeast running into huge sums of money, on the other hand a phobic militaristic regime is established to quell the disaffected voices striving to protect their identities. This is done not so much with the intention to improve their lot but with the intention of assimilating diverse peoples by taming and asserting control over their territory. The monies for development rarely reach the intended populations as corrupt local politicians and government officials siphon them off towards their personal aggrandizement. A large sum of it also enters the hands of the insurgent organizations that run parallel governments via "taxation" which is but a euphemism for extortion thereby making a mockery of the State machinery. This is ironical given that nation-building uses the language of modernity that is premised upon the Enlightenment ideals of delivering reason, progress, justice, equality et al. Frantz Fanon suggests that a transfer of affect in the colonial situation occurs, whereby the white colonizers "inject" or "deposit" their anger into the colonized who are then forced to expel it in self-destructive ways (Kelly, 2005).

> The settler keeps alive in the native an anger which he deprives of outlet; the native is trapped in the tight links of the chains of colonialism... The native's muscular tension finds outlet regularly in the bloodthirsty explosions in tribal warfare, in feuds between sects, and in quarrels between individuals. (Fanon, 1962, p. 54)

Drawing from this, it may be argued that the internecine clashes between various communities in the Northeast cannot be attributed to border disputes, tribalism and ego battles alone, but also to a neurosis that results from the transfer of affect, that of "injecting" anger onto the natives by the Indian State in the form of excesses of military operation and human rights violations. The Northeastern insurgents, who are caught in the tight links of Indian hegemony, "deposit" their anger onto spheres that manifest into explosive intra- and inter-community violence.

Having exhausted its efforts in playing the role of the social reformer and benevolent master, the State resorts to the use of its repressive apparatus in the form of police and military that unleashes a reign of terror. On March 4 and 5, 1966 the Indian Air Force bombarded civilian inhabited areas of Aizawl, razing them to the ground, in the name of preserving national security. The Armed Forces (Special

Powers) Act (1958), which is implemented in many states of the Northeast to contain insurgency, epitomizes the most repressive military regime in independent democratic India. It is an extremely draconian legislation which provides even non-commissioned officers to operate with impunity in a "disturbed" civilian area as it empowers them to:

- Fire upon or use other kinds of force on civilians even if it causes death.
- To arrest anyone without a warrant and with the use of "necessary" force who has committed certain offences or is suspected of having done so.
- To enter and search any premise in order to make such arrests.

This legislation has brought untold misery to innocent civilians leading to myriad human rights violations in the form of arbitrary detention, torture, rape, ransacking, and extrajudicial killings. The major components of the nation-state such as the bureaucracy, the judiciary, the police and the army are indeed descendants of their colonial predecessors. The ubiquitous presence of security forces in civilian areas and their acts of transgression has come to hamper the citizens' engagement with their day to day activities as much as the non-state militiamen do. Under this scheme of things, disturbing questions arise as to who and what is being secured by the presence of security forces.

In conclusion it may be stated that this paper is not meant as a call to revert to traditionalism as the means to undo the ravages of modernization and nation-building. This is neither possible nor feasible because modernity is intricately enmeshed with tradition in the everyday existence of citizens in India. Attempts at mono-nationalisms and sub-nationalisms based on region, language, religion, ethnicity, etc. can be fatal as manifested in the form of rightwing nationalism, which has reared its ugly head in modern India. The policy of integration at the cost of subsuming minority identities is clearly not without problems and should be abandoned. At a moment when a post-national condition is being debated, it would be worthwhile to chart out alternative trajectories of encountering modernity. This should be based on rapprochement and a quest to include and impart education on the various histories that have been elided in the grand narratives of Indian historiography.

Endnotes

1. The idea for this paper came from a seminar conducted by A.B. Akoijam and Ravi Vasudevan at Jawaharlal Nehru University in 2009. Acknowledgment must also be made of Ira Bhaskar for her suggestions. An earlier version of the paper was presented at the University of Cordoba, Spain and the writer is thankful for the responses which further shaped the paper.
2. Produced and directed by Atma Ram in 1972.

References

Althusser, L. (1971). *Lenin and Philosophy and Other Essays*. New York and London: Monthly Review Press.

Baruah, S. (2004). *Between South and Southeast Asia: Northeast India and Look East Policy*. Guwahati: Ceniseas Paper 4.

Bhabha, H.K. (1994). *The Location of Culture.* London, New York: Routledge.

Marx, K. and Engels, F. (1959). *The First Indian War of Independence 1857-1859.* Moscow: Foreign Languages Publishing House.

Chatterjee, P. (1999). Nationalism as a Problem in the History of Political Ideas. In *The Partha Chatterjee Omnibus.* New Delhi: Oxford University Press.

Fanon, F. (1952). *Black Skin White Masks*. New York: Grove Press.

Fanon, F. (1961). *The Wretched of the Earth.* New York: Grove Press.

Gramsci, A. *Selections from the Prison Notebooks*. New York: International Publications.

Nandy, A. (2002). *The Romance of the State: And the Fate of Dissent in the Tropics.* New Delhi: Oxford University Press.

Nibaran, B. Insurgency in the North-East. In B.C. Bhuyan (Ed.) *Political Development of the North-East,* Vol. 2. New Delhi: Omsons Publications.

Oliver, K. (2005). On "The Good Infection". *Parallax,* Vol. 11, No. 3, 92-93.

6

Developing Bastar: The Dandakaranya Project

Saagar Tiwari

> The area is large, with sufficient living space and good scope for development. It is rich in mineral and forest wealth. It is under-developed and hence lends itself to planned development. It is under-populated and when developed can absorb more population without adversely affecting the interests of the local people. In fact, no other area in India could offer the same scope for large-scale reclamation and colonization.
>
> Preface, *Development of Dandakaranya*[1]

I

Before partition, the region which became East Pakistan had a population of 12 million Hindus. By the mid 1950s, over 4 million Hindus from this region had crossed over to India and many more continued to do so. The Government of India was hard pressed to solve the resettlement problem of these East Bengal Refugees (officially called "East Pakistan Displaced Persons" or EPDPs). Of this number, about three million were settled in West Bengal making it "over saturated". About 3 lakhs were in camps and shelters and the remaining were settled in the states of Tripura, Manipur and Assam. Large amounts had to be spent on the care and sustenance of an ever-increasing numbers of refugees. Since about 70 per cent of the refugees were agriculturists, massive efforts were made to secure cultivable land in all parts of the country in order to settle them. States other than West Bengal, Tripura and Assam were approached to assist in finding land but only about 100,000 acres "of marginal and sub-marginal quality" land could be made available. There was also the challenge of development that would require the clearance of forests, the provision of tractors, communication, irrigation, anti-malarial drives and other health measures so as to make these areas habitable. Yet experts stated that the sheer number of displaced persons meant that even if 100,000 acres were fully developed, it would "help only in touching the fringe of the problem"[2].

To tackle the problem effectively, the Government of India started "to think in terms of a big area, backed up by a definite scheme, in which these (displaced) people could be settled"[3]. Furthermore, it was thought that since the refugees pouring in from across the border were mostly "Namsudras", who were sturdy agriculturists, "settling [them] in suitably developed areas should not present a difficult problem"[4]. Thus, in the mid 1950s, work began on the Dandakaranya Project, arguably the largest agricultural colonization operation undertaken in independent India. The novelty of the idea was such that it led the Union Rehabilitation Secretary to remark that initially, "it was just a conception and it was expected that ideas will crystallize as time goes on"[5]. A brief outline of its history would be useful.

Early History of the Dandakaranya Project

The concept was formulated by T.T. Krishnamachari, the Union Finance Minister and Ram Murthy, Advisor to the Planning Commission. In November 1956, Krishnamachari felt that the problem of Rehabilitation of East Pakistan Displaced Persons was "going out of hand"[6] and it was necessary to tackle this influx in a more determined manner. Thereafter, in a letter to the Chief Minister of M.P., Dr. K.N. Katju, the Union Minister of Rehabilitation, Mehr Chand

Khanna wrote that the matter was "becoming more and more difficult with their [the refugees'] continued influx". For resettlement purposes, he suggested the exploration of

> possibilities of utilizing the large tract of land that covers the eastern portion of Sircars (Andhra), the western and the south-western portion of Hyderabad, the Bastar State in Madhya Pradesh and the Jeypore zamindari in Orissa...the area in question constitutes a contiguous block of about 80,000 square miles and a large part of it is covered with primeval forest. It is contemplated that half of the area should be left as forest and the population of the rest raised by 4 millions, of which half may be the local Adivasis and the other half displaced persons.[7]

This area was understood to be the Dandakaranya forest of the *Ramayana*. Hence, this scheme was named the "Dandakaranya Project". According to Chief Administrator A.L. Fletcher's note, operations were to begin with the reclamation of small areas near the existing centre of population with a view to setting up refugee settlements. This was to deal with the immediate problem of dispersing the camp population in West Bengal. At the same time a skeleton master plan was to be prepared within 6-8 months for the integrated development of the region, to be followed by a final master plan which was to include schemes of communication, irrigation and power, agriculture and animal husbandry, commerce & industries including mineral development and health. More colonies would be built for displaced persons and tribals once the area had been opened out with the progress of developmental schemes.[8]

To consider this scheme, a committee known as the AMPO Committee was set up with the Secretary, Ministry of Finance, H.M. Patel as its Chairman and the Rehabilitation Secretary, the Agricultural Secretary, the Joint Secretary (Planning Commission) and the Joint Secretary (Home Ministry) as members. The Committee met for the first time on 22nd January 1957 and discussed the scheme.[9]

The "Tribal" Question: Debate within Official Circles

From the beginning, a serious debate pervaded the state establishment over the Dandakaranya scheme. In the second AMPO meeting, representatives from the Home Ministry expressed apprehensions over the impact of this scheme on the tribal population. They raised three main considerations as to how this project was likely to affect "prejudicially the interests of the existing tribal inhabitants of this area"[10]. Passages below discuss this debate.

Firstly, the area identified for the project was largely inhabited by tribals, who, because of their "ingrained aversion...to any organized scheme of development"[11] and "conservative attitude of mind" were unlikely to react favorably to any scheme of development, particularly if it involved the introduction of a foreign element into the population. It was feared that this would lead to an intensification of tribal prejudices.

Secondly, ordinary laws did not apply to these "Scheduled Areas", whose inhabitants enjoyed special protection. Hence, the representatives of the Home Ministry argued that "if displaced persons were settled in these areas, either they will have to be treated as backward people or, in the alternative, the tribal people will have to be deprived of some of the protection which is given to them"[12]. Also, the grants-in-aid given to the State Governments under Article 275 of the Constitution were intended specially for the welfare of Scheduled Tribes. The introduction of extraneous elements not entitled to the benefits of these grants could lead to many complications.[13]

And lastly, it was feared that the pattern of mixed colonization which was being planned would give the tribals an impression that they were being either squeezed out or assimilated.[14]

It was, therefore, suggested that these aspects of the matter be carefully considered. The Chairman stated that the Rehabilitation Committee of the Cabinet had directed the

AMPO Committee to ensure that necessary safeguards for tribal inhabitants be kept in mind while schemes of development were worked out. On the main points raised by the representatives of the Home Ministry, the Committee decided that,

> The question of legal complications will have to be tackled on a different footing. So far as the protective laws are concerned, they will have to continue for some time not withstanding the introduction of extraneous groups....As regards the financial assistance by the Centre under Article 275 of the Constitution, they too will have to continue and the quantum thereof probably may require to be increased because the entire area is bound to be more activised through the introduction of extraneous elements...Similarly, the fear that tribes may be squeezed out, has to be removed by positive action to ensure that such a contingency does not arise. They will call for intimate co-operation between the state Government and the authorities in charge of the development of this area. Such co-operation need not be ruled out as impracticable and given such co-operation, the fears may turn out to be less formidable than they appear.[15]

This led to the argument that the difficulties were "not insurmountable" but it was necessary was "to proceed with caution." During the next meeting of the Committee on 30th January 1957, the Chairman argued that "this area could not remain backward for all times to come and even at a certain amount of calculated risk, the development of this area has to be embarked upon in the larger national interest."[16] The decision was taken to appoint an Executive Officer to undertake the work of survey and formulation required by the scheme. In September 1957 A.L. Fletcher was appointed as the Chief Executive Officer.[17]

Beginning in 1956, extensive surveys were carried on in Malkangiri *tehsil* of Koraput district and Kalahandi district in Orissa and the Paralkot and Narayanpur divisions of Bastar district. The suitability of these areas on several parameters like soil, rainfall, potential irrigation sources, connectivity with nearest rail-heads, kind of forest, cost of reclamation and other infrastructure development etc were considered. Following these preliminary surveys, the realization dawned that the "possibilities could certainly not be so unlimited as envisaged in the original concept."[18] Some officials pointed out that even in the definition of objectives, the emphasis had varied slightly at times betraying a lack of clarity.

Many officials felt that in view of these varying statements it was difficult to say whether the scheme involved the reclamation of land for the tribals "also" or the reclamation of land was primarily for the resettlement of refugees and "the advantages accruing to the local population were in terms of communication, public health and opportunity for employment."[19] These apprehensions were soon moderated by the work of Fletcher. He described the scheme as involving the co-coordinated development of the region in which rehabilitation of displaced people from East Pakistan is "merely a part and not the whole."

Fletcher also argued that the evolution of an integrated regional plan could not be rushed. It involved "a number of surveys, the collection and evaluation of data, the appreciation of many factors and master planning by experts." However, since the rehabilitation of displaced persons was a case of extreme urgency, it should be taken up forthwith and pursued with all vigor, while planning for regional development would simultaneously continue. Initially, the scope of the Dandakaranya project was to be limited to approximately 25,000 sq. miles: the operational area would thus be the Malkangiri taluka of Koraput district, a portion of the Kalahandi district and the whole of the Bastar district.

Moreover, Fletcher felt that it would be necessary to undertake surveys of soil conservation, irrigation, etc since even preliminary contour maps were not available. It was, therefore, very important that these surveys be taken up first. The planners encountered a massive challenge because despite its great possibilities, this area also presented a number of difficulties – such as "lack of adequate means of communication, of marketing facilities, chronic labor shortage, malaria and wild animals" – which needed to be overcome.

Along with the above mentioned considerations, Fletcher also emphasized that the "psychological aspect" also be kept in view. He argued that the settlers should only be brought when the internal roads and sites of habitation were cleared, houses put up and ration depots opened. The settlers could also take part in the lighter operations of reclamation, community works and housing etc in the neighboring settlements. According to him, "There should be tangible evidence of a promising future. The settlers should be made to feel and realize that they have been brought to a land of promise in the development of which they have an important and vital role to play"[20].

A further element confounding the situation was added by the Tribal Welfare Department (TWD). It agreed with the general consensus that it was unlikely that the region would indefinitely remain backward as there was no alternative to planned development of these areas. However, the TWD also suggested that at least during the initial stages, locating new village settlements must be done in consultation with the local people and only in such places that were not objected to.[21] Additionally, the TWD argued that the most important safeguard desired for the tribals was the provision of land for them. It suggested that "the best method by which we can ensure that the tribals will not be pushed out from this area would be to provide for 50% of the reclaimed land for tribals. Without this the tribals would never believe our good intentions and the danger of his complete extinction will also not be removed"[22].

The files of the Rehabilitation Department also reveal some interesting view points. In particular, from the notes of S.V. Ramamurthy, considered the original mind behind this plan, the following extract reveals certain crucial underpinnings of the planning exercise,

> In Dandakaranya, there is need for townships which link villages, provide amenities of life for middle classes who can stimulate agriculture in villages around and give scope for intelligent professional people to live in the area and help in its development. Round the township, villages have to spring up without denuding the needed forests... The social reclamation of these tribesmen is as vital a problem as the land reclamation in forests. Social conditions are a reflection of the natural conditions. The way to reclaim the forest dwellers is to change their economy from a forest economy to a village economy. For this, land for cultivation, water for irrigation, village settlements with houses, roads and provision for education and health have to be brought to being, these having a central township. Cottage industries may spread from township to villages.... Communications throughout the area are necessary as also a mass attack against malaria. If this be provided, life from neighboring plains will spread to the area. This is not only good for the utilization of the natural resources of the area but also good for the hillmen. *Hillmen cannot progress unless they have the example of plainsmen as to how to progress economically.* [Emphasis added]They need to be warned from shifting cultivation which is ruining the forests and denuding the soil. [23]

This passage provides a brilliant example of the vision of the "intelligent professional people" in opposition to the "hill tribesmen". While the former were harbingers of development, the latter were bereft of any agency and consequently became the "sites" of development. What is remarkable here is the idea of desire and the need for converting the "tribal" into a "peasant". The entire economy of the tribals depending upon the forests was to be changed into a settled/sedentary "village economy". The forest dweller became the target for "social reclamation". Equally significant is the implied idea of the "push" which was imperative to break the stagnation and inertia of the hill tribes ("Hillmen cannot progress...economically"). At least at the level of discourse, this sounds almost a variant of the "white man's burden", expressed through the binary of hillmen and plainsmen.

The infusion of outside elements was justified by stating that these areas were "sparsely populated" and had an "acute shortage of manual labor"[24]. There was also a dearth of artisans and of skilled labor of all kinds. Hence, once settled, there was massive scope for employment of displaced persons in local work. According to planners, in the interest of the future development of the Dandakaranya area, it was "essential to fill this void by importing artisans and skilled labor, for current needs, and training others, local as well as settlers, to meet the expanding demands"[25]. Moreover, the planners argued that since it was unlikely that this region would remain backward indefinitely, there was no alternative to planned development of resources.

With such an agenda firmly in place the inaugural meeting of the Dandakaranya Development Authority (DDA) was held at Jaisalmer House, Delhi on the 14th and 15th of October, 1958. In his inaugural address, the Union Rehabilitation Minister said that in the implementation of the Dandakaranya Scheme, the Authority was to keep three factors firmly in mind. These were: (a) the problem of rehabilitation had to be dealt with on an emergency footing. He was not in favor of any unnecessary risk being taken but desired that the displaced persons be settled as early as possible; (b) the relief expenditure on families staying in the camps amounted to Rs. 2.25 lakhs per day. This was held to be "entirely wasteful and should be stopped as early as possible and the amount utilized on productive work" and; (c) moral degradation caused by atmosphere in the camps.[26]

After raising these issues, the Minister argued that for these families to be genuinely rehabilitated they had to be taken off the dole and immediately put to work. Thus, the Dandakaranya Scheme had to provide work to displaced persons as otherwise, the families themselves would not move unless work was offered. Hence, one of the primary tasks of the Authority was to provide work in the Dandakaranya Scheme.[27] Sometime earlier, in a meeting held at Calcutta on the 3rd and 4th of July 1958, important decisions were taken which included the closing down of camps in West Bengal by July 1959. Plans had been drawn for the absorption and employment of at least 20,000 families in Dandakaranya by this deadline.[28] About 12 companies or 3 battalions of Dandakaranya Development Corps were to be formed from this workforce and entrusted with implementing this project.

The ultimate solution to dilemmas on the "tribal" question was expressed by the planners as follows,

> Development of this area is necessary and will have to come. The extreme school of thought which wanted that the tribal area should be left alone as contact with civilization means necessary degradation has now lost ground. We would want that the tribals live in prosperity, in better hygienic conditions, diseases like yaws and malaria are eradicated and roads etc., built in the area but at the same time we also want to ensure that the tribal is not completely ousted, that he continues to get preferential treatment as laid down in the constitution and that the mode of life and cultural and social pattern of tribals is preserved to the utmost extent. The best plan for the development of the area, is, therefore, one in which foreign element was introduced to the minimum extent possible and this should have been restricted to the industrial area primarily. But in view of the national problem of East Pakistan displaced persons this seems to be difficult. The displaced persons have also to be provided. The proper approach to the scheme, therefore, should be that it is a scheme for the integrated development of this area, the emphasis being primarily on the tribals. Incidentally the said development will offer opportunity for the resettlement of displaced persons also. The present emphasis on the early settlement of displaced persons will require to be shifted to slow and planned development of the area for the tribals.[29]

II
Dandakaranya Perspective Plan

Let us now examine the Integrated Development and regional planning exercise of the Dandakaranya region. Its beginnings can be traced to the files which formed the source material for the preceding section. Discussing the potential for development of the Dandakaranya region the planners declared:

> Being a backward and, at the same time, a rich area, the scope for development is great. The area, however, bristles with many major problems, all of which must be tackled in an integrated and planned manner if a sound socio-economic structure is to emerge.... The intention is to undertake this planning with the aid of a staff of regional planning experts. The preparation of the master plan, which is to take three years, will involve a number of surveys, investigations and researches by planning experts in collaboration with the State Governments and the Project's own development experts. An attempt will be made to produce a skeleton plan in a year's time. The execution of the Master Plan may well start in the Third Plan period and extend over several years.[30]

Exactly how this "rule of experts" reconstituted the Dandakaraṇya region is what we shall now examine.

The Public Accounts Committee of the Fourth Lok Sabha lamented the absence of a long term perspective plan for the Dandakaranya Region while reviewing the progress made in the project. The preparation of this plan was entrusted to the Town and Country Planning Organization (TCPO) of the GOI, and after much delay the plan document was finally prepared by the TCPO in association with the Multi-level Planning Division of the Planning Commission.

The resultant dossier was the "Perspective Plan for Dandakaranya Region" (1975).[31] It is a massive dossier containing 12 chapters spread over 709 pages which outlines the planners' grand vision for the region. The text is replete with tables, maps and a detailed program which sought to radically transform the region between 1975 and 1990. Here, the earlier area of Dandakaranya was expanded to include Baudh-Khondmal (a.k.a. Phulbani) district of Orissa which was now clubbed together with Bastar, Koraput and Kalahandi (Dharamgarh and Sadar sub-divisions) districts. The entire region had an area of 85,500 square kilometers and contained a population of 50 lakhs, of which nearly 53% were tribals.

The dossier analyzed the prevalent state of development and human welfare, the problems related to development, also providing an assessment of the potentialities and future actions to be initiated. It surveyed the prevalent trends and conditions in diverse sectors such as agriculture, animal husbandry, forests, mining & minerals, industrial development, water resources, power, transport & communications, urbanization and settlement system and social development. On each of these themes (dealt in separate chapters), the planners extensively prescribed their development strategies and operational machineries. Though the schemes contained in this dossier could never be fully implemented on the ground, the DPP in itself provides us a fascinating model of a high modernist intervention by the state.

Recommended Drive Towards Industrialization

The dossier vigorously argued the case for massive industrial development of the Dandakaranya region. Echoing the spirit of the times, industrial development was justified by the DPP planners as the panacea for ameliorating the "backwardness" of the area. The planners stated that industrial development was skewed in the region as it was predominated by the small scale industries which constituted about 99% of the total industrial units and 62.9% of the total industrial work-force in the region.[32] Among the small scale industries, non-resource based ones had the largest number of units followed by agro-based industries. On top of this, industrialization was not uniformly distributed in the region. Koraput and

Kalahandi districts were relatively better developed industrially as compared to Phulbani and Bastar districts.

An integral part of the planned strategy for was the role assigned to external agency in providing a "push" to the process of industrialization. The planners argued that initially the private sector was likely to be skeptical in starting new ventures due to the backwardness of the region. Therefore, initially the role of the vanguard was to be played by the Centre and/or its agencies till the private sector gradually follows up as the infrastructural facilities and "external economies" become progressively available. With regard to the respective roles of the public and private sector, the planners argued that while the public sector could play a very important role in setting up basic industries, and start units producing machinery, machine tools, agricultural implements etc., the private sector could subsequently join in and play a vital role in setting up intermediate and consumer goods industries largely based on forest, live-stock and agro-resources of the region.[33]

The DPP planners conceived the industrialization of the Dandakaranya Region in different stages extending over a period of about two decades. They stated that to achieve "an organic, diversified and balanced development of the Region," it was necessary to have a strategy for a gradual process of development with a clear perspective of objectives to be attained in a short period (of say 5 years) and the long period (of 15-20 years).[34] In view of these considerations the strategy for industrial development was to be divided into two stages *viz.* (i) short term and (ii) long term. These divisions were not to be inflexible or monolithic in nature but rather interdependent and complimentary.

The short term strategy was to concentrate on creating agro-cum-need based consumer goods industries that had short gestation periods, were labor intensive and employed simple technology. On the other hand, the long term strategy was designed to involve a gradual movement towards medium and large scale industries along with the development of socio-economic infrastructure. Care was to be taken, however, that intermediate level technology must be applied in fields such as steel plants, around which machine and machine tool making units may be established. This was to ensure adequate employment was generated for the local population.

The planners placed the Dandakaranya region within an overarching framework of "backwardness". They declared

> "Backwardness" is a relative term. Backwardness of a region directly implies non-development or under-development of essentially the resources both economic and human. The level of development of the resources only reflects the level of availability of social and economic infrastructures. The poor development of a region like the Dandakaranya, which abounds in natural resources but yet suffers a pronounced backwardness is only due to non-provision of infrastructural facilities.[35]

The DPP plan team agreed that though some developments had taken place in certain pockets of the region and its surrounding areas, the fruits of development had not been transmitted to the interior. Apart from lack of infrastructure, the blame was put on the absence of an organizational framework, within which human social or economic activities could function. Explaining their significance and mutual interdependence, the planners said that "economic organization enables inflow and out-flow of goods and services, social organization helps to establish codes of conduct and behavior, marriages, family ties, social institutions, and cultural traits-all stem from the social organizational set up"[36].

Highlighting the contrast, the planners stated that while there were industrially well developed pockets in the region with strong organizational setup, such as the Bailadilla Iron-Ore Project, there also existed large tracts like the "Abhujmars" which quite literally meant "the lands not known yet". These developed pockets were to act as "regulators". They were mainly the centers of primary and secondary activities. The latter by their very nature were of a higher hierarchical status "with good network of infrastructures and propulsive forces of development"[37].

The planners concluded that their analysis of the development of different sectors in the Dandakaranya Region had revealed a paradoxical situation of poverty amidst plenty. They lamented the situation in which despite having ample natural resources for the development of agriculture, forestry, trade and commerce, industries etc., the predominantly tribal population of the area (53%) belonging to "a different economic and cultural milieu" were not in a position to take up development of the resources "in the manner in which it has been conceived for other parts of the country"[38].

Modernization was clearly not bearing the desired results and the planners admitted at the end of the dossier that "the present modes of developmental effort" implemented thus far to develop this "backward area...do not seem appropriate as they do not invite participation of the tribal population in the developmental process"[39]. They even sounded alarm bells by declaring that

> If the tribal population and tribal culture should not break up and vanish altogether ultimately there(sic) it is very necessary that the development strategy for this area must have basically a people's approach instead of a technological approach. We may go even further to say that the people's approach must predominate and if necessary even at the cost of a technological slow down.

Outlining this "peoples' approach", the planners argued for giving attention to agriculture and forestry. They said that the tribal population now was very well versed in agriculture although production remains at a marginal level. Forestry practices too, according to them depict a similar pattern, where the tribals were engaged in collection of firewood and minor forest products (such as *sal* seed, *mahua* flowers etc.) and where the perceptible failure lay in non-exploitation of industrial timber. These primary sectors in the Dandakaranya region hence, suffered from lack of inputs, both of knowledge and of tools and plants. The situation could, however, be modified and the planners recommended that,

> Any developmental program, therefore, must attempt in the first instance to support and encourage the present pattern of activities of the tribal population, namely in agriculture and forestry with a firm emphasis on vocations. The change has to take place in a considerably shorter period than what has taken place elsewhere if the tribal population has to be brought by a telescoped program which can squeeze in 4-5 years what is normally achieved in a 10 year period.[40]

This approach essentially meant that investments were to be made in "parallel sectors" such as irrigation, rural electrification, and provision of inputs such as fertilizers, distribution services and marketing facilities. The planners stressed that these had to be provided on a priority basis. However, there was a crucial qualification that "such a development strategy does not... preclude projects which may have to be taken up to meet national priorities, commitments and demands, such as the establishment of a pulp-paper complex at Barsur, Bauxite mines in Koraput area or a pig-iron Plant at Bailadilla."[41]

It was predicted that if the above approach was implemented the situation would change dramatically. The resultant increase in agricultural production and forestry output will automatically attract a lot of other linked industries, both in the private and public sectors, as a result of availability of raw materials and opportunities of processing them at low costs. The planners envisioned that

> It is during this phase that the tribal population can be taken to the next stage of learning about working in industries and improving their lot by shifting from the primary to the secondary sector. Appropriately oriented training programmes, provided they are taken up in advance, will make it possible to have sufficiently trained man-power available in that area to man the new industries and it may not be necessary at that

> stage for outsiders to be brought in. Advance action is necessary for training the educated sections of the tribal population in industrial production and management. The increase in per capita income which the development of agriculture, forestry and industries will bring about, will mean higher consumer demand and opportunity for consumer industries to be established in the region. Textiles, ready-made garments, and a host of daily needs industries will move in providing the population better services and amenities.[42]

The planners advocated that this strategy was to be followed during the 5th, 6th and the 7th Five Year Plans after which the consequent development was likely to arrest the withdrawal process of the tribals and would "bring the tribal population into the mainstream of development within the country."[43] By the end of the twentieth century it was expected that this area would catch up with the rest of the country in regard both to its pattern of economic activities as well as its per capita income.[44]

Conclusion

The Dandakaranya Project emerged out of a contingent situation which had developed after the partition of India. Being a novel idea with no similar predecessor, the planning and implementation of this developmental cum refugee-resettlement project was a massive challenge for the state officials. When the ball started rolling, several contradictions emerged, chief among which was the potential inimical impact on the tribal population inhabiting this area. A debate ensued which was resolved in favor of the project work continuing and preparation to complete a long-term master plan for the integrated development of the region. The voice of the tribals hardly found a place in the entire exercise.

Other issues which cropped up were those of forests and administrative liaison which too were decided in a similar fashion using the same conceptual grid. The planners used strategies such as statistics and the employment of binaries to justify their case.

The Perspective Plan on the other hand serves as an exemplar of economic reductionism. The vision of the high modernist planners greatly simplified and rationalized the landscape and the tribal body of the Dandakaranya region. These were now inserted into the framework of the overarching logic of nationalism and developmentalism. "Nature" was turned into "natural resource" and the population turned into "human resource" whose quality had to be increased. The ostensible justification for doing so came from the logic of welfare and the new emergent discourse on citizenship through which the "backward" tribals were to be "integrated" into the body-politic. Throughout this process, the industrial exploitation of the region's natural resources remained high on the planners' agenda.

Endnotes

1. National Council of Applied Economic Research (1963), *Development of Dandakaranya*, NCAER, New Delhi, p. v.
2. A note for the Rehabilitation Committee of the Cabinet by Dharam Vira in F. No. B-1(a)-22, Rehabilitation Department, GOMP, 1959. pp. 11-14.
3. Copy of D.O. letter No. 10079-PSF/56 dated 13th November, 1956 from Finance Minister, India to Deputy Chairman, Planning Commission in F. No. B-1(a)-22, Rehabilitation Department, GOMP, 1959. p. 7.
4. A note for the Rehabilitation Committee of the Cabinet by Dharam Vira in F. No. B-1(a)-22, Rehabilitation Department, GOMP, 1959. p. 12.
5. A note on Dandakaranya Scheme – its implications and its organizational pattern in F. No. B-1 (a)-22, Rehabilitation Department, GOMP, 1959, p. 137.
6. Copy of D.O. letter No. 10079-PSF/56 dated 13th November, 1956 from Finance Minister, India to Deputy Chairman, Planning Commission in F. No. B-1(a)-22, Rehabilitation Department, GOMP, 1959. p. 7.
7. D.O. No. 200/PSMR/45-S, dated Jan 24, 1957 in F. No. B-1(a)-22, Rehabilitation Department, GOMP, 1959. p. 1.
8. *Ibid.*, p. 22.

9. A note on Dandakaranya Scheme – its implications and organizational pattern in F. No. B-1(a)-22, Rehabilitation Department, GOMP, 1959. p. 138.
10. F. No. B-1(a)-22, Rehabilitation Department, GOMP, 1959. p. 8.
11. D.O. Letter No. 573 RR dated 21/22 January, 1957 from B. Sivaraman, Chief Secretary, Orissa Government to V.T. Krishnamachari, Vice Chairman Planning Commission, in F. No. B-1 (a)-22, Rehabilitation Department, GOMP, 1959. p. 39.
12. *Ibid.*, p. 39.
13. *Ibid.*, pp. 39-40.
14. *Ibid.*, p. 40.
15. F. No. B-1(a)-22, Rehabilitation Department, GOMP, 1959, pp. 9-10.
16. A note on Dandakaranya Scheme – its implications and organizational pattern in F. No. B-1(a)-22, Rehabilitation Department, GOMP, 1959. p. 138.
17. *Ibid.*
18. A note on Dandakaranya Scheme – its implications and organizational pattern in F. No. B-1(a)-22, Rehabilitation Department, GOMP, 1959, p. 140.
19. *Ibid.*
20. A note on Dandakaranya Scheme – its implications and organizational pattern in F. No. B-1(a)-22, Rehabilitation Department, GOMP, 1959, p. 145.
21. *Ibid.*, p.148. It went on to suggest the following safeguards:
    (1) The schemes should not affect the classification of the area as scheduled and consequent benefits derived in the shape of grants under Article 275 of the Constitution.
    (2) At least in the initial stages existing agricultural holdings should not be acquired nor should existing villages be disturbed. Local inhabitants should be consulted wherever possible as the scheme is implemented.
    (3) The TWD should be adequately represented in whatever organization is set up for the purpose of implementation of the scheme.
22. *Ibid.*
23. S.V. Ramamurthy's note dated 13-11-56 in F. No. B-1(a)-22, Rehabilitation Department, GOMP, 1959. pp.7-8., pp. 9-10, emphasis added.
24. A note on Dandakaranya Scheme – its implications and

organizational pattern in F. No. B-1 (a)-22, Rehabilitation Department, GOMP, 1959, p. 144.

25. *Ibid.*
26. 'Draft Proceedings of the inaugural meeting of DDA at Jaisalmer House, Delhi on 14th and 15th October, 1958' in F. No. B-1 (a)-27, Rehabilitation Department (East Pakistan), GOMP, 1959, pp. 106-108.
27. *Ibid.*
28. *Ibid.*, p.46. By conservative estimates, the number of families for whom employment was to be provided under differentt heads were: Road work (2,000), Reclamation (3500), Construction of new villages (6000), Irrigation works (2500), Construction of Project buildings (1000), Operation of trucks (700), Distribution of consumer goods (650), Dairy Units (500) and Production centers for brick, tiles, doors windows etc.(1000). This totaled up to almost 18000 families.
29. A note on Dandakaranya Scheme – its implications and organizational pattern in F. No. B-1 (a)-22, Rehabilitation Department, GOMP, 1959, pp. 149-150.
30. *Ibid.*
31. Town and Country Planning Organization (1975), *Perspective Plan for Dandakaranya Region*, TCPO, Ministry of Works and Housing, GOI, (mimeo.), Henceforth, DPP.
32. DPP, p. 225.
33. DPP, pp. 303-304.
34. DPP, p. 305.
35. DPP, p. 574.
36. *Ibid.*
37. *Ibid.*
38. DPP, p. 694.
39. DPP, p. 695.
40. *Ibid.*
41. DPP, p. 697
42. DPP, p. 698.
43. DPP, p. 699.
44. DPP, p. 700.

Contributors

Anirban Nigam studies at the School of Art and Aesthetics, Jawaharlal Nehru University, New Delhi

Nandita Badami studies at the Centre for Political Studies, School of Social Sciences, Jawaharlal Nehru University, New Delhi

Manisha Tripathy Pandey is Associate Professor, Department of Sociology, Jamia Millia Islamia, New Delhi. Her recent publication is *Globalization and the Indian Urban Middle Class: The Emerging Trend* (New Delhi: Uppal Publishing House, 2010)

Neikolie Kuotsu studies at the School of Art and Aesthetics, Jawaharlal Nehru University, New Delhi. His research interest lies in the intersection of cinema, aesthetics, postcolonialism, technology, globalization, and power discourse and has recently completed a research titled *Korean Wave in 'Northeast' India: Rethinking Regional Film Cultures*.

Paresh Chandra is a student/activist, located in the University of Delhi, where he studies literature. He is part of a students' group called "Correspondence" which seeks to engage in dialogue with various individuals and groups, so as to try and theorize the possibilities of an authentic transformative politics in the university.

Ravi Kumar teaches at the Department of Sociology, Jamia Millia Islamia, New Delhi. His publications include *The Politics of Imperialism and Counterstrategies* (co-edited, Delhi: Aakar Books, 2004); *The Crisis of Elementary Education in India* (edited, New Delhi: Sage, 2006); *Global Neoliberalism and Education and its Consequences* (co-edited, New York: Routledge, 2009); *Ghetto and Within: Class, Identity, State and Politics of Mobilisation* (Delhi: Aakar Books, 2010)

Saagar Tewari is a student of the Ph.D. programme at the Centre for Historical Studies, Jawaharlal Nehru University. He is working on post-colonial developments in the Bastar region.

Savyasaachi teaches at the Department of Sociology at Jamia MIllia Islamia. Some of his recent works include *FRA 2006: In Who's Interest; Truth Telling Beyond Neo Liberal Education;* and *Radical Insistence, Resistance and Resilience - the Political Economy of Words*